"Elisa gently explores the work of (___ ___ our lives, the fruit of the Spirit. Fille ___ practical exercises, *Fruitful Living* will bring encouragement and help as you collaborate with God's Spirit to bear fruit."

—**Amy Boucher Pye**, author of
Transforming Love: How Friendship with Jesus Changes Us

"As my friend Elisa Morgan reminds on the following pages, *Fruitful Living* isn't about perfectly executing a to-do list. It's about ruthlessly attaching to a person—Jesus. And what He started in you He will finish. You can count on it."

—**Michele Cushatt**, author of *A Faith That Will Not Fail: 10 Practices to Build Up Your Faith When Your World Is Falling Apart*

"With vulnerable authenticity, compassion, and wit, Elisa reveals the rewards and the 'costly choice' of being discipled by God. Each chapter ends with an invitation to dig deeper into Scripture and Get Growing. Relevant and worthy of repeated readings as a personal devotional or a group study, *Fruitful Living* comes alongside hearts ready to receive the Gardener's gift of a fruitful legacy."

—**Xochitl Dixon**, contributing writer for *Our Daily Bread* and *God Hears Her*, and the author of *Waiting for God* and *Sacred Strides: Walking in the Power and Presence of the Holy Spirit*

"Refreshing. Thought-provoking. Biblical. Challenging. If you long to live a life that matters, read this book. Elisa Morgan skillfully reveals the secret to leaving a legacy that will far outlast your achievements. It's a fresh look at the fruit of the Spirit and it will provide the tools for making a heart change that results in positive action. Read it the first time on your own; then gather a group of friends to study, discuss, and implement a plan for personal and spiritual transformation."

—**Carol Kent**, founder and executive director of SpeakUp Ministries and author of *He Holds My Hand*

"Just when God's weary workers need a fresh word, the marvelous Elisa Morgan comes forth to lead us into inspiration that enchants, excites, and delights. With her splendid new book *Fruitful Living*, she takes us into God's fruitful garden to let the Orchard Keeper Himself plant, prune, and grow a bounty of rich spiritual fruit to render in us a life that matters. So taste and see."

—**Patricia Raybon**, a regular contributor to *Our Daily Bread*, author of *God Is Our Help* and the award-winning Annalee Spain Mysteries

"This book is your guide to grow a meaningful life—one filled with love, joy, peace, patience, kindness, goodness, faithfulness, gentleness, and self-control. Elisa's approachable and relatable stories combined with biblical truth show us how to discover and cultivate a purposeful life worth living, even in the hardest of seasons and worst of circumstances."

—**Laura L. Smith**, author of *The Urgency of Slowing Down* and *Holy Care for the Whole Self*

fruitful living

Growing a Life That Matters

Elisa Morgan

Our Daily Bread
Publishing.

Requests for permission to quote from this book should be directed to: Permissions Department, Our Daily Bread Publishing, PO Box 3566, Grand Rapids, MI 49501; or contact us by email at permissionsdept@odb.org.

Comments from social media survey respondents used with permission.

Scripture quotations, unless otherwise indicated, are taken from the Holy Bible, New International Version®, NIV®. Copyright © 1973, 1978, 1984, 2011 by Biblica, Inc.™ Used by permission of Zondervan. All rights reserved worldwide. www.zondervan.com.

Scripture quotations marked ESV are taken from the ESV® Bible (The Holy Bible, English Standard Version®), copyright © 2001 by Crossway, a publishing ministry of Good News Publishers. Used by permission. All rights reserved.

Interior design by Michael J. Williams

ISBN: 978-1-64070-363-6

Library of Congress Cataloging-in-Publication Data Available

Printed in the United States of America
25 26 27 28 29 30 31 32 / 8 7 6 5 4 3 2 1

Contents

Longing for a Life That Matters

I pulled back the covers and lowered my fifteen-pound Jack Russell Terrier, Mia, to the carpet. Over ten years old now, she woke eeeeeaaarrrllly each morning, insisting on a potty break. (My husband calls this "checking her pee-mail.") Mia's errand completed, I returned to the kitchen, where I punched a pod into the Keurig and stood looking out the window at the day while mentally reviewing my calendar.

Not much there, really. Writing. Grocery store. Walking Mia. More writing. In my current season of life, my hours are mine for scheduling. I can assign most appointments in the neat slots on my phone's calendar, including work, friends, grandma time, and even reading and walking. Most days I'm fulfilled, even happy. Occasionally I wriggle against the sensation of boredom as it slips through the cracks into my awareness. And yet this particular morning, staring out the window while my coffee dripped in the background, I wondered about the meaning of my life. What legacy would I leave? Who would remember me and for what? (Research shows that our names are only remembered three generations after we die.[1]) Was there anything in my efforts that really was pleasing to God?

These are not new thoughts. I asked these same questions as a scared single girl exploring education and vocation options, as a newly married woman dipping my toe into coupledom, as a frantic mom dashing between kids and work and EVERYTHING, and as a mother of teens-turning-to-young-adults who suddenly seemed to want pretty much nothing from me (except in all the emergency moments when they needed me and my husband and more than what any human could offer).

One of our greatest questions in our lives focuses on our purpose. Contribution. Impact. Influence. Legacy. In short, what difference do we make? And one of our greatest answers to this question is that we want to grow a life that matters. This drive toward purpose motivates us to produce achievements. We climb the career ladder, nurture a family, add titles and letters after our names, chair committees, write books, create art, develop a social media platform. Achievements mark our contribution on this planet.

Until they don't. When we slip down a rung or two at work . . . when our family matures beyond needing us . . . when we're no longer invited to lead, our books go out of print, and social media ignores us . . . how do we measure our mattering then?

"As Henri Nouwen frequently reminds us, achievement is not the same thing as fruitfulness," writes Ron Rolheiser. "Our achievements are things we have accomplished. Our fruitfulness is the positive, long-term effect these achievements have on others. . . . When we die, while we may well be eulogized for our achievements, we will be loved and remembered more for the goodness of our hearts."[2]

Here's where the fruit of the Spirit comes in. If we want to describe a life that matters, one with purpose and meaning and contribution, we'll turn to the evidence of these characteristics that God offers us in Scripture.

Look at the words. Just the words.

Love. Joy. Peace. Patience. Kindness. Goodness. Faithfulness. Gentleness. Self-control.

When we focus on those words—just the words—that compose the classic fruit in Galatians 5, we pause. Something stirs inside us. Loving? Yes, please—I want to be. Patient? Absolutely. They're attractive qualities. We want them. We want them in us, and we want to reproduce them in others. We long for them in our days and our nights and in all the moments in between. And long term, in moments when we look out at the length of our lives, we yearn for the legacy of a fruitful life that memorializes these characteristics as our life's central offering. Oh, that others would speak of us with these beautiful adjectives and, in so doing, see Jesus in us!

But how? Here's where it gets challenging, right? After all, we're not Mother Teresa or Jesus. We're us. Humans. On the run. In the trenches. Under stress. Many of us are moms and grandmoms. Some of us are wives. Daughters and granddaughters making our way. How can we grow such qualities in ourselves or in those we love? Growing a fruitful life of love, joy, peace, patience, kindness, goodness, faithfulness, gentleness, and self-control seems beyond our grasp.

That's because we hold two misunderstandings about the fruit of the Spirit. We think spiritual fruit is about being nice. Plus, we think it's all up to us to produce. Neither is true.

The fruit of the Spirit is not about being nice. The fruit of the Spirit is about being like Jesus. Jesus was *always* loving, joyful, peaceful, patient, kind, good, faithful, gentle, and self-controlled. But these qualities didn't always wear the peeling of "nice" in His interactions. His love was acted out in telling a prostitute to stop sinning and religious leaders to quit making faith harder than God intended it to be. His kindness led Him to touch an outcast leper during a day when such an action was strictly prohibited. His peace put Him to sleep in a boat with disciples in the middle of a storm out at sea. Such moments don't define "niceness." But they were definitely fruit filled.

It's not about being nice. But the *being* part is true. Rather than a list to perform, these godly characteristics are the result of God's work in us, transforming our inner beings into what He always intended us to be: like Him.

Neither is the fruit of the Spirit all up to us to grow. It's not our job to produce these qualities in our lives or in the lives of those around us. Fruit production is God's job. In his Discovery Series booklet *A Fresh Look at the Fruit of the Spirit*, Con Campbell puts it this way: "We must understand that these characteristics are produced by the third person of the Trinity. He is the agent, the source and the power that grows the fruit."[3] The fruit of the Spirit grows when we let God live these qualities in us and through us as we grow in relationship with Him. Fruitful living results from an ongoing attachment to God while still being human.

Ready to grow a life that matters?

We'll begin with the work of grasping the definition and purpose of God's fruit—in general. Then we'll move on to understand each individual fruit both biblically and practically. For each spiritual fruit, I've assigned a literal fruit as a metaphor to help us remember its essence. Finally, we'll focus on how we can attach ourselves to God as the Source of fruitful living in order to grow a life that matters. Each chapter also includes a "Get Growing" section to help apply concepts personally in everyday life—or for use in a study with friends.

Throughout the book, I'll be including comments and insights from you—readers who responded to a survey done through social media. Over the years, I've learned that books are better when I include more viewpoints and insights.

Fruitful living is about growing a life that matters by peeling past the "niceness" of Christianity and getting down to the honest truth of letting God grow us to become more like Jesus. God makes it simple. We make it hard. As much as we want to grow a life that matters, He longs to grow such a life in us. So let's get growing!

PART 1

Fruit Matters

CHAPTER 1

What Is Spiritual Fruit?

You're in the produce section of your neighborhood grocery store. Just for a minute, lay your list aside and look. In bins and boxes, piled high, stacked neatly, arranged in alternating bands of color, are fruits of every imaginable flavor and type. Focus on the fruit.

Apples mirror your reflection in their polished surface. Within their crunchy fruit, their seeds make a star-shaped design when cut in half horizontally. Grapefruit exude a tangy, sweet aroma, their skin thick and spongy. Bananas perch delicately, bunched by fives and sixes, yellow skin dotted with brown age spots. Strawberries wear their seeds like a sweater. Pineapples guard their sweetness with a prickly exterior. Coconuts challenge any fruit eater to break through their shell to the good stuff.

Fruit. Varieties of smells and shapes and sizes. All nutritious. All sweet. Each distinct. Each unique.

Fruit is the result of growth. It's the evidence that a plant or a vine or a tree has been cared for to the point of reproducing. Spiritual fruit is what results in our lives when we root ourselves in a relationship with God. When we live a life connected like this with God, He grows His nature in who we are, and fruit

15

results. Love, joy, peace, patience, kindness, goodness, faithfulness, gentleness, and self-control.

Consider the opposite for a moment. The New Testament book of Galatians lists certain qualities resulting from a life disconnected from God. The writer, a follower of God named Paul, lists "sexual immorality, impurity, sensuality, idolatry, sorcery, enmity, strife, jealousy, fits of anger, rivalries, dissensions, divisions, envy, drunkenness, orgies, and things like these" (Galatians 5:19–21 ESV). Not too pretty! Not produce we'd pinch, smell, and take home to The Fam for the week. They are obvious, says Paul (v. 19), and his list isn't even complete, just illustrative (v. 21). These characteristics result from a life lived on our own, separate from God and stuck with only the best we can be.

Ah, but then Paul describes the results of a life lived in connection with God. A life lived in a healthy direction that makes a difference today for tomorrow. A fruitful life. The fruit, the produce, of the Spirit is "love, joy, peace, patience, kindness, goodness, faithfulness, gentleness, self-control" (vv. 22–23 ESV). Here are attractive, appealing attributes we want in our lives, the lives of our children and grandchildren, and the lives of those in our world.

However, the fruit of the Spirit aren't like a checklist of items we pick up at the grocery store. They're not something we're commanded to bear. Rather, they are qualities others observe in us when we're in relationship with God—and not all believers will bear all the fruit all the time. At times, some of us will be more patient, more peaceful, or more loving than others. Moreover, in addition to Paul's list of fruit in Galatians, other God-grown characteristics are mentioned elsewhere in Scripture—qualities like perseverance, humility, and thankfulness that display the Spirit's work in our lives.[1]

The fruit of the Spirit are those godlike qualities that make us look like Him. Rather than *doing* words, they are *being* words. They describe His nature exhibited in our personalities. When we plant ourselves in a relationship with Jesus, day in and day out, He produces His characteristics in us. The fruit of the Spirit is what we look like when we're like Jesus.

Such a description can be unsettling. Looking and acting like Jesus? That might be a very good thing—but will our own personality fade away? Will God replace the "me" we know with some saint-like replica of what we believe Jesus to be? Will our edgy enthusiasm be tamed to a controlled warmth? Our tough determinism melted to a driven discipline? We picture a robot-like being—only holier. We pull back and wonder, Will I even recognize myself if I live such a fruit-filled life? Will I still be me?

Remember, the fruit of the Spirit is not about being nice. The fruit is God's characteristics. But His characteristics are exhibited in our unique personalities. Being like Jesus means showing love, joy, peace, patience, kindness, goodness, faithfulness, gentleness, and self-control in exactly who we are—not something other than ourselves but fully and authentically ourselves.

Peace in your own skin might look like a calm version of a caffeine addict, whereas in the skin of your friend it may look more like a way laid-back chill. Joy might appear as stillness in you but more like a whooped-up party in your sister.

For me, this "God's fruit in my own skin" concept comes home when I look at my major life heroes—and how far short of their image I feel I fall. Take Mother Teresa. Compassionate. Giving. Fearless. Sacrificial. Content with possessing nothing. I look at the life she lived, immersing herself in the power of Jesus amidst poverty and offering hope without ceasing. Then I think about my own attitude when I get stuck forty-five minutes in traffic, or when my husband doesn't move his snack plates from the sink to the dishwasher.

Mother Elisa looks very little like Mother Teresa.

But hey, we're so hard on ourselves! Yes, there are way too many moments when "ugly" emerges in my life responses. But there are actually occasions when I find myself engaged by a friend's need to the point that I race to the hospital to be at her side and don't seem to notice I haven't eaten or had anything to drink or even gone to the bathroom for hours. Or I notice someone's favorite shirt is soiled and so I throw in an extra load to prepare it for the next day's needs. Or I notice I'm extra grumpy *before* I lose my tongue and don't actually verbalize what I so much want to say.

Maybe I don't look like Mother Teresa all the time. But maybe— just maybe—I look a little bit like Jesus now and then because I'm rooted in a relationship with Him and He's growing me to be like Him.

Wait a minute—I'm saying that it's harder for me to look like Mother Teresa than it is to look like Jesus! Well, of course. It's always harder for us to repeat the offering of another person than it is to be the best me we can be with the help of Jesus.

Love, joy, peace, patience, kindness, goodness, faithfulness, gentleness and self-control. These are the fruit of the Spirit. These are God's qualities exhibited in our personalities. These are what we look like when we look like God.

Get Growing

1. Read Galatians 5:13–25. Paul contrasts the acts of the flesh with the fruit of the Spirit. How do they differ? Where do you struggle with the "acts of the flesh"? Now consider Paul's list of the fruit of the Spirit. Which most appeal to you?

2. Think about how peaches grow from a peach tree, strawberries from a vine, pineapples from a bush. Each fruit looks unique and yet grows as a result of its attachment to the source of growth. Mentally flip through the people you know who model spiritual fruit. Maybe your mother-in-law, your sister, a neighbor, a coworker, or a pastor. Name the fruit you can see most plainly in each person's life. How does each fruit change from personality to personality? What does this exercise tell you about what spiritual fruit might look like in your personality? How about in your children, your grandchildren, your spouse, or your dearest friend? What did you learn?

3. God's character grows in you as you "plant" yourself in Him. Have you ever made such a decision to plant yourself in God? You can pray a simple prayer like this:

   Dear Jesus, I want to be like You. I need the help and the promise You offer. I need the hope of being connected to You and Your perfection in this crazy world. I can't do life by myself without messing it up. Please save me from myself so I can be the best me I can be by being in a relationship with You. And, as I "plant" myself in You, will You please grow these qualities that look like You in me? I long for a life that matters and that makes a difference in my family and my world. I realize that happens when these qualities are growing in me out of a relationship with You. In Your name, Amen.

> "The fruit of the Spirit is love, joy, peace, patience, kindness, goodness, faithfulness, gentleness, self-control; against such things there is no law." (Galatians 5:22–23 ESV)

The fruit of the Spirit is . . .

- The outward demonstration of the Holy Spirit working in my life. (Amy)
- The evidence of a life that has been given to Jesus and is growing in holy beauty and intimacy with Him. (Glenda)
- Not just knowing but living out love, joy, peace, patience, kindness, goodness, faithfulness, gentleness, and self-control. (Jessica)
- The characteristics of Jesus. (Amy)

CHAPTER 2

What Is the Purpose of Spiritual Fruit?

Why does the Bible refer to the qualities of God-likeness as *fruit*? What's the purpose of this metaphor?

A nursery owner sets out to sell peach trees. She considers her approaches. She might peddle pictures of leafy saplings bound in burlap sacks. She might display a four-color catalog opened to pictures of peach trees throughout the year—bare-branched, flowering, fruiting, and postfruit. But what really sells a peach tree is the peach it produces: pungent, deep orange, fuzzy skinned, dangling from the branches. You can see it. You can smell it. You can touch it. You can taste it. It's the peach that sells the peach tree.

God is the master marketer. He packages Himself in wrappers of fruit: love, joy, peace, patience, kindness, goodness, faithfulness, gentleness, and self-control.

Fruit markets. Fruit sells God to a world hungry for truth, for hope, and for life. At first that might seem like a sneaky or even manipulative thing. It's not. Physical fruit is something we know. It beckons us to take a bite. Likewise, spiritual fruit arouses our interest with its lure of impact. We're familiar with its amazing names. God is so much bigger, but He meets us in the language, words, and qualities of our longing for meaning so that we might want Him and what He wants.

Fruit is the external result of an internal relationship. It's the dressing that beckons others to want to know the God we represent. Paul writes in Romans 13:14, "Clothe yourselves with the Lord Jesus Christ, and do not think about how to gratify the desires of the flesh." Fruit looks good! It smells good! And when we get to know fruit-filled people, we discover that fruit tastes good as well. Like bright oranges standing out against the green leaves of a tree, the fruit of the Spirit announces to a starving world, "Here is food! Here is life! Come and find a way out of exhaustion and discouragement. Come and meet God."

My friend Bonnie is a generation above me. Years ago I met her through my husband's work. More than most folks I can think of, Bonnie markets the character of God. Her passion for Him is contagious. Because of the fruit I see in Bonnie's life, she has made me want more and more of God.

From the moment Bonnie greets me with "Elisa!" whether in person or on the phone, I feel loved by God Himself. When she asks about the details of my life, I experience an acceptance that demonstrates the deepest kind of patience. Throughout my now-grown children's lives, Bonnie sent each of them birthday cards carrying five-dollar bills—a kindness my kids came to count on. And faithful? Oh, my. Bonnie has consistently offered care and prayer through all the seasons of my marriage, my mothering, and my life. Bonnie attracts me to the hope I can have in God through the fruit of His character displayed in her life.

One year in particular, I struggled deeply with my relationship with my mother. I grew up in a broken home. My parents divorced when I was five, and my mother—bless her heart—battled alcoholism all the years of her adult life. While she knew God as a young child, she avoided Him in her adult days. In my thirties my personal work included healing from the confusion of my childhood and, specifically, a very codependent relationship with my mother. I had been more of a mother to her than she had been to me.

When I learned my mother had cancer, what I experienced wasn't the conclusion of our mother-daughter journey; it was more like panic that I'd be responsible for her eternity. I felt hopeless, loveless, and prayerless when it came to my mother and her hereafter.

I turned to Bonnie. I asked Bonnie to pray for my mother because I'd worn out the topic before God. She did. Daily. Faithfully. From time to time, she'd check in and ask me for topics, words, or concerns. What did I want her to pray for my mother? I told her to please pray that my mother would see her need for God and that she would desire heaven. I waited. Bonnie prayed.

The week my mother died, she called to tell me that she'd remembered two poems, both spiritual in nature. One was "L'Envoi" by Rudyard Kipling—all about heaven. The other was "Footprints in the Sand." At last. My mother had come to see her need for God and had begun to desire heaven.

Bonnie's prayers have kept God before me, guiding me to Him and to the attributes He longs to grow in my own life. Fruit in one life markets the hope of Jesus to another life.

I know I'm not the only one who needs an up-close-and-personal example in order to grasp how God's character would look in my life. We all ask the questions: How does patience work with a cranky toddler or sulky teen? Where does a sweet voice come from when it's a struggle just to stay calm? Can we still grow the fruit of kindness if we say no to distractions in order to get things done? How?

Lisa mentions a friend who endured deep financial need and yet always opened her home to others. Her children's friends were always over, and there was at least one adult, if not more, just hanging out. Lisa's friend fed everyone who was at her house, every day.

Janet muses, "My spouse is quick to forgive, no matter the hurt. His patience amazes me."

Allison's in-laws modeled rich fruit to her. "My mother-in-law suffered with ALS, and even though bedbound near the end of her life, she never stopped smiling. And my father-in-law never complained as he cared for her."

Ann recalls a pastor who shepherded several churches. "Everywhere he went he left a mark on lives. Everyone wanted him to do their family members' funerals because of the caring words he shared."

Cindy deeply admires a friend with a chronic, severe health issue. "She so radiates a faithful and full-of-fruit life that I come away from every conversation encouraged, so blessed. She loves lavishly, always pointing others to the Father. Her faith is humbling. It's staggering that she could be so full of hope when she has many reasons to question God (which she does, with a giggle as she says it), railing at the unfairness of her diagnosis, her limitations. Because she has lived a life of faith, her fruit is ripe and heavy, beautiful in its maturity."

We look at others and want real help. Others look at us and want the same, not some "nice" version of faith that they can never hope to have. When they see the patience, the faithfulness, the gentleness of Jesus in the life of a Christian, people outside the faith are attracted to God. They reach and grab for the promise offered by God's fruit in our lives, hungry for the message it sells.

So I'll repeat: Fruit markets. Fruit draws people to God and the hope they can find in Him. And it distinguishes good from evil. Jesus, speaking to His followers about the difference between true and false prophets, said, "Watch out for false prophets. They come to you in sheep's clothing, but inwardly they are ferocious wolves. By their fruit you will recognize them" (Matthew 7:15–16). Love. Joy. Peace. Patience. Kindness. Goodness. Gentleness. Faithfulness. Self-control. Wrap your life in these qualities, and let God offer His character through you to the hungry in the world around you.

Oh—one more thing. Resist the urge to glitz, spin, and alter your life's advertisement for Jesus. The fruit of the Spirit is wrapper enough for the truth of God's character extended through us. We tend to think, "Oh, it's up to me to make God look good!" "I must improve His image before others!" "It's my job to clear up the confusion out there about who God is!"

But sticking an "All Natural" label on an apple doesn't make the apple natural—it just is . . . or isn't if it's plastic. And it's the same with spiritual fruit. We might be tempted to plaster a smile on a sour face, hoping to portray an image of joy. Or gloss over the inevitable pain of life when a friend contracts cancer. Or guarantee a happy life in exchange for a child's faithful trust in Jesus. But while spinning the truth is an acceptable practice in advertising, we're wise to avoid it in spiritual fruit marketing.

Spiritual fruit is fruit with a spiritual purpose. It markets God to a world hungry for the hope they can have in Him.

Get Growing

1. Go get an apple, a peach, or a lemon—any piece of fruit—out of the fridge or the fruit bowl on your kitchen counter. Cut it open and look at its parts. Skin. Body. Seed. Depending on your selection, what lessons can you learn from the physical qualities of this fruit?

2. Now think about someone you know whom you respect for how they seem to know God. What qualities drew you to this person at first? How did such characteristics inspire you to want more of what that person possesses?

3. Love. Joy. Peace. Patience. Kindness. Goodness. Gentleness. Faithfulness. Self-control. Scan this list while asking yourself, Which of these fruits do my children need to see in my life in order to see the God I love? Which ones does my spouse need to see as an advertisement of the hope I have in God? What about your friend at work—which fruit might market God's love to her?

4. Contemplate the point about spin in advertising. Are there ways you've decided it's up to you to handle how God looks to others—improving or protecting His reputation? When you realize He is best seen in the fruit of the Spirit expressed in your personality, where do you sense the need to peel off unnecessary outsides of your life and get down to the simple, pure fruit?

5. Read Romans 13:14. What would it mean for you to put on Jesus Christ as you would put on clothes?

Dear Jesus, I am changed by the understanding that the purpose of Your fruit is to draw others to the hope and help they can have in You. I also realize that I'm sometimes tempted to "add on" to Your clear qualities and probably end up muddying Your image rather than modeling it. Help me to relax in who You really are and let You grow these

*fruits of Your character purely and simply in my
days without embellishment, trusting You with the
results. In Your name, Amen.*

"Clothe yourselves with the Lord Jesus Christ."
(Romans 13:14)

The purpose of the fruit of the Spirit is . . .

- God living through His children to show who He is to the world. (Ann)
- The light of Jesus shining through us in our everyday encounters. (Dee)
- To attract others to Jesus. (Donna)
- To show others that Christ is the best answer to any question. (Iris)
- To bring Jesus-like qualities to the world around me. (Jill)
- To make people want to know more about Jesus. (Stacy)

CHAPTER 3

How to "Get Growing": A Deeper Look

Back in my days of raising "littles," I used to count the minutes until I could plop down on the couch with my two cherubs and zone out in front of *Sesame Street*. After hours of getting kids in and out of car seats, cutting up sandwiches into bite-sized morsels, lap-reading, and nose-wiping, I finally rested.

I remember an episode where Telly Monster had surrounded himself with all kinds of healthy foods. In between bites of carrot, Telly stretched and groaned, urging his pudgy body upwards. When asked what he was doing, Telly replied, "I'm trying to grow!"

I relate to Telly Monster. I'm one of those petite-type women who never really bloomed past fifth grade. In fifth grade I was a giant at five feet two inches. I wore a size five-and-a-half shoe. I towered over the boys yet to come into their prime. I can remember focusing on eating healthy and exercising, but every time I backed up against the door jamb where I'd marked my height, the measurement remained unchanged.

Today I measure half a shoe size larger and one inch taller (must have been all those doughnuts in college). There's not really much any of us can do to change our genetic makeup of height and shoe size.

While there are certainly moments when I'm stunned that I'm the grown-up (You mean *I* have to figure out what's for dinner *every* night?) and I'd rather remain childlike in my responsibilities (Can't someone else pay this bill for me?), in general I *want* to grow in all areas of my life. You too, no doubt. I mean, it's kind of like we were *born* to grow. We're propelled forward. There's something exhilarating about getting our driver's license, learning to navigate a new city after a move, sharing our thoughts in a book club, mastering tech skills, or preparing an entire dinner with side dishes and getting it on the table—hot. Growing is good.

But what role do we play in growing the fruit of the Spirit in our lives? Why is it that our best efforts are about as productive as those of Telly Monster on *Sesame Street* (and me in fifth grade)?

Here's why. Think how our genetics determine the appearance and size of our physical bodies. Our efforts can influence the outcome, but in the end, our height, shoe size, eye color, and so on are up to how we're designed. Similarly, while we have a role to play in our spiritual growth, the result is ultimately up to God.

By our own efforts we'll grow fruit of the flesh at best. Becky discovered, "Shame and trying harder doesn't work." Bethany learned, "I've found that when I try to do it on my own, it becomes about me." Gayle admits, "When I am thinking only of myself, fruit doesn't grow. It turns brown and ugly in my heart."

We can't make ourselves look like God. Only God can do that. Only God can reproduce His nature in us. Writing to the early church, Paul said, "I planted the seed, Apollos [another worker] watered it, but God has been making it grow" (1 Corinthians

3:6). When we receive the seed of hope into the soil of our lives and begin a connected relationship with God, He lives inside us. We get His spiritual DNA. Like a twenty-four-hour gardener, God tills the soil of our lives until we begin to grow qualities that resemble His nature. By His interest and effort in us, we grow into holy orchards.

With all this said, we do have a role in our growth. Just as we can't grow spiritual fruit without God, God can't grow spiritual fruit in us without us. Our job in spiritual growth is to cooperate with the Gardener.

Here's what cooperation looks like in our lives.

Be receptive. A seed can't germinate in clay-packed soil. Our job includes staying soft so we can receive the seeds God wants to plant in our lives. Admittedly, being receptive can be a challenge at times. We resist the intrusion of someone else's agenda. What if we're not in the mood for God to grow us? What if we'd rather slump down on the couch and binge the latest Netflix series? What if we *like* the dullness of our days because there's a kind of predictable safeness there?

When we recognize such resistance, we're wise to tell a friend, say a prayer, or just gently remind ourselves that God is not out to get us. He simply wants us to grow the same way we want ourselves to grow: into people who make a difference and live lives that matter.

Endure pruning. Horticulturalists have long touted the benefits of pruning—but not in a haphazard way. The many good reasons to prune include removing dead, diseased, or damaged wood to ensure continued good health; improving flowering and fruit production; and shaping young plants to a desired form.[1]

Jesus explained to His disciples that pruning would be part of their growth: "I am the true vine, and my Father is the gardener. He cuts off every branch in me that bears no fruit, while every branch that does bear fruit he prunes so that it will be even more fruitful" (John 15:1–2). Part of the growing process involves cutting off what is diseased or no longer necessary or even what is taking nutrients that are needed elsewhere.

I find it much harder to endure pruning than to be receptive to new growth. Pruning can be painful, right? We don't want to part with some stuff that may actually need to go. Sarcasm is fun! Oh, it isn't being like Jesus? Hmm. Grudges? Oooh, but they're so self-vindicating! But are they like Jesus?

You get the point. Someone has said, "You're not in a growth zone if you're in a comfort zone, and you're not in a comfort zone if you're in a growth zone." Ouch.

Stay connected. Jill shares, "I tried [to grow spiritual fruit] for too long and became a human doing and not a human being. I am learning to do what the Word tells me to do and that there are no magic formulas. God wants a relationship with me, as unique as I am. He made us all different for a reason, and I believe He grows us individually. He is so gentle and wise. What works is letting Him lead me and teach me. He produces the fruit in me as I seek to keep Him first in my heart and life."

We can't grow spiritually if we detach from the source of our growth. Jesus said, "Remain in me, as I also remain in you. No branch can bear fruit by itself; it must remain in the vine. Neither can you bear fruit unless you remain in me" (John 15:4). A leaf doesn't continue growing once it's pulled from a branch. When we stop hanging out with others who care about growing, we'll probably stop growing too. When we let week after week slip by without going to a church service or a study group or even spending some time opening up ourselves to God in prayer or Bible reading, we'll likely shrink rather than grow.

Ready to get growing? It's up to God to grow His fruit in our lives, but it's up to us to cooperate with Him. Just as we can't grow spiritual fruit without God, God can't grow it in us without us.

Get Growing

1. Read 1 Corinthians 3:6. What is your role in fruit production? What is God's?
2. In what ways is God growing His nature in your life? What is He doing to develop His characteristics in your unique personality?
3. Read John 15:1–5. How can you better cooperate with the Gardener who wants you to grow? In what area are you resisting rather than receiving? Where might you be avoiding rather than enduring His pruning? And in what ways is it difficult for you to stay connected to the Vine?

Dear Jesus, thank You that growing in these qualities is a two-way, mutual process. You don't require that I lay down who I am and become robotic in my responses. Instead, You invite me to join Your work in me and, through me, in the world. I choose to cooperate. In Your name, Amen.

"Other seed fell on good soil. It came up and yielded a crop, a hundred times more than was sown." (Luke 8:8)

33

We "get growing" when we . . .

- Offer God rich soil. (Alexandra)
- Follow the Holy Spirit's prompting by being obedient. (Allison)
- Spend time in God's Word and around seasoned believers. (Carol)
- Be a willing participant. (Christy)
- Keep attached to the Vine and close to the Vinedresser. (Gayle)
- Pray. The closer you are to God, the more you are filled with the fruit. (Meg)
- Stop beating ourselves up when we fail. (Iris)

PART 2

The Fruit of the Spirit

CHAPTER 4

Love

Our Always-in-Everything Commitment

Grapes. *The quality of a grape is directly related to its host vine. Grapes abide in their vine. Unattached from their source, they wither. Grapes offer an example of commitment through the easy and hard times of life. Vine growers report that the sweetest grapes come from the most stressed vines.*

Ｆirst on the list: love. Easy, right?

In life, love starts out with our love for our parents. We fall in love with Mommy and Daddy and somehow believe they will always be the center of our universe.

Then there are siblings. Best friends in some seasons. Competitors in others. Sometimes lifelong companions, as they can end up being the longest relationships in our lives.

Twinkly seasons of dating and young marriage. The early months and years are ecstatic. Every glance satisfies. Every exchange rewards. In many, many marriages, the magic remains long into advanced seasons, developing into a mature and mutual love.

Bestie friendships. The sense that you can complete each other's sentences, drop everything and help when needed, be one another's plus-one, and in general, give and receive understanding, forgiveness, and the freedom to be yourselves.

How about motherhood? Our initiation is divine. Sure, there is the inevitable pain, but no matter how wrinkly, red, or ridiculous our baby might appear to others, to us that tiny one is spectacular. No duration of labor or surgery or fear of the unknown ahead could hold our hearts back from the complete delight of loving this little child who has become ours through birth or adoption.

And grandparenting? Pure joy! Someone said that the best thing about grandparenting is hugs and taillights. Yup!

Among all the qualities of God's character produced in us by His Spirit, love seems the most natural, second nature, and easiest to both offer and receive.

Until some unexpected evening when our darling husband calls, late for the millionth time on the very night we've scheduled dinner with a girlfriend and we're utterly dependent on him to take over so we can take off. In that moment our previously unending sense of love evaporates like water off a car hood on a Tucson summer afternoon.

Or until that precious baby whimpers to a full-blown howl at 3:00 in the morning, and no one is there to take a turn because Dad is traveling—or never stayed around to sign up fully for fatherhood. Oh, we love that baby more than our own life, but the desire for sleep seduces us into a rage that tears our attention from loving our child the way we intend.

Or the call to caregiving reveals surprising facets of our being. A brother, a parent, a spouse, a friend, or a child who requires ongoing care calls us to invest with unending love. At times we rally and marvel at our ability to offer ourselves. In other moments, the day in and day out, the unending nights, the supervision of medications and meals and body care require an investment many of us recoil from.

Love. Indeed, so often it seems the easiest of all qualities to model. Except when love is hard. And it can be hard, can't it?

Let's get real about love. It can be *hard* to love people. Love means handing over the remote control when we'd rather keep it, getting up to respond to a request just when we've settled into a comfy spot, speaking in a balanced tone when we'd rather scream, opening our heart to listen when we'd rather tumble out our own feelings and needs, or waking up when we'd rather sleep. Yep, it's hard to love people.

Because people are hard to love. Spouse people, parent people, neighbor and friend people, even baby and child people. They all seem to want what we don't always want to give. Sometimes they are grateful and appreciative when we go out of our way for them. Sometimes they reciprocate. But there are also many moments when they are picky, critical, snippy, and we wonder why we bothered trying.

So how can we grow this fruit of love in our lives—in *everything*? It's not a big deal to love when it's easy. But when it's hard, then what? Are we to plaster on the martyr mask and grit our way through? Should we smile submissively and pretend to love the man we're so very ticked at? Is that what love looks like—nice, nice, nice all the time, even when it's hard? What would Jesus do in the everyday when it's hard to love hard-to-love people?

First Corinthians 13:4–8 contains the most famous, defining description of love in history. "Love is patient, love is kind. It does not envy, it does not boast, it is not proud. It does not dishonor others, it is not self-seeking, it is not easily angered, it keeps no record of wrongs. Love does not delight in evil but rejoices with the truth. It always protects, always trusts, always hopes, always perseveres. Love never fails."

As one resource puts it, this love is "based on sincere appreciation and high regard."[1] It's unconditional and unending.

Rereading the verses, we see the other eight fruits of the Spirit thread through these verses, don't we? Ah—more evidence that spiritual fruit is best evidenced in clusters, a variety of qualities that exhibit Jesus's character in our personalities.

Along these lines, Cindy shares, "Some of our family members have turned away from God, and as a result, our deep spiritual connection has been severed. I have been hurt and confused because a part of their rejection is also a rejection of all that I have poured into them and how I have loved them. Throughout these past couple of years, I have felt God encouraging me to love them more than ever before, to be more intentional. In many ways, my love for them is calling me to exhibit each of the other fruits of the Spirit in winsome ways to woo them back to faith. The fruit of love is the foundation for all the other fruits as we interact with others."

I've been married nearly fifty years now. In the early years of my marriage—and before, when we were dating—I thought love meant anticipating each other's every need and rushing in to fix something before it was even broken. I thought love meant feeling the same way about political issues and agreeing on everyday matters like what time to turn out the lights and how many pillows to put on the bed. I couldn't imagine arguments as a part of a loving relationship, or selfishness influencing whose turn it was to get groceries, or criticism layered over how to discipline our children.

Was I ever wrong!

In real life, decades into marriage, two children, their spouses, and three grandchildren later, it's clear to me that all this very confusing stuff *does* fit into the world where love lives. Choosing a commitment to love in the "everything" of such skirmishes teaches us that love can coexist with conflict and even grow stronger.

Glenda echoes my learning. "Love is so much more than a feeling. My husband has dealt with addiction for most of our marriage, and it was hell on earth for decades while he was active in his addiction. God brought me to a place of total reliance in His love—a love I knew I could rely on and would never change. I have been able to deal with old wounds and experience healing in the midst of this journey, which has given a whole new definition to how love is lived out in my marriage."

I imagined that motherhood would produce Elisa-cloned children who held my views, made the choices I would make, and expressed the emotions I feel. Not. Instead, we have real, individual children who have grown into real individual adults, unique and distinct from my definition and from me. But in choosing my commitment to my children, I find my heart has grown a love I didn't realize was possible, shaped by the challenges and deepened through diversity.

Same with my grandchildren. And the same with my friendships, which morph and mature with each passing year. Long ago my friendships were about discovering and knowing each other and being safe in the acceptance of being known. Today my friendships are still about being known and accepted, but there is an honest recognition of one another's flaws and diminishments that my friends and I embrace as much as the bright discoveries of our youth.

An example of love comes from a long-ago member of our family. Hang in here with me for a minute, will you? It involves BeeBee the hamster. Yep, a hamster.

It was about 9:30 one night when my daughter, Eva, then about thirteen, shrieked at me from her bedroom down the hall.

"Mom! Come heeeeeerrrreeee! *Now!*"

I ran in response to find my daughter standing rigidly above her hamster's cage, eyes wide and mouth agape. "BeeBee's having babies!" she announced.

Sure enough, seven-week-old Bee Bee, an occupant in our home for only the past two weeks, was a mother. Eleven (did you get that—*eleven*) half-inch-long, wormlike babies were mouthing the air about her, searching for food. Ahhh, I thought, bless your heart, BeeBee.

In the days that followed, BeeBee ate—that she might feed her babies. She slept, sprawled out for her babies to reach—that she might warm her babies. She shoved pine straw in womblike piles—that she might protect her babies. One morning we peeled back the towel that covered the cage to find it empty. Gasping, we searched for the itty-bitty babies. I pictured National Geographic moments where wild animals eat their young, and I panicked with worries of just what BeeBee had consumed for breakfast.

And then I discovered BeeBee with her brood, safely snuggled inside her plastic hamster ball. She had scooped them all in with her and sat, happily feeding all eleven. As I peered down at her, she dislodged herself from her spot to greet me and struggled through the ball's opening, dragging eleven mouths along.

"Oh, BeeBee!" I whispered. "You're doing such a good job!"

This was choice. This was commitment. (Actually, maybe it was just instinct. After all she was just a hamster. But when I consider such devotion, I saw love.) This was love: a committed choice to be there . . . in everything.

When it's hard to love hard-to-love people, the fruit of love helps us in the "everything" moments of life. I think back to my selection of grapes as a physical reminder for the spiritual fruit of love: "The quality of a grape is directly related to its host vine. Grapes abide in their vine. Unattached from their source, they wither." God is the source of all the spiritual fruits. He is the source of love. As John writes, "God is love. . . . We love because he first loved us" (1 John 4:16, 19). Because He loves us in the everything of life, we can love others. He shows us the way.

In the everything moments, love is a choice. God chose to love us. He didn't have to. He wanted to love us, so He chose to love us. And we choose to love others. Sure, sometimes it doesn't seem like a choice, like when we fall in love with our baby, our husband, or even a best friend. That's more of a "can't help but feel it" emotion, isn't it? But later, when the newness of love wears off and we're caught in a relationship, it is the *choice* of love that continues. And when we find ourselves in relationships we hadn't realized we'd chosen—neighbors, in-laws, coworkers, and dependents—love wakes up and chooses all over again, intentionally this time.

Love is also commitment—in everything. God is committed to us, no matter what. Nothing—absolutely nothing—can "separate us from the love of God in Christ Jesus" (see Romans 8:38–39). Love stays when it wants to go. It accepts when it wants to reject. It forgives when doing so seems to make no sense. It does what it doesn't want to do when it doesn't want to do it. It gets above the "I can't stand this person" moments and, squinting, forces itself to look at that someone the way

God looks at him or her, as flawed, yes, but filled with potential. Love is a commitment to keep choosing to love . . . even when you don't feel like it.

And thus, godlike (BeeBee-like, if you will), we choose, we commit, and we *practice* this kind of love in everything and get better at it bit by bit. Notice I didn't say *perfect*. We won't ever be perfect at love. But we can be better. More honest in our love. More consistent. More expressive. Quicker. When we give a backrub, text a friend some words of encouragement, plant a smooch on the cheek of our kindergartener, or wash the communion cups at church, we are practicing love. When we practice love, we improve.

In many life moments, love comes easily. But when love is hard, we're helped by recalling what love is. Love is the fruit that gets us past being-nice politeness to love's real offering when it's hard to love hard-to-love people.

Get Growing

1. When is it most difficult for you to love someone? Try to be specific about what circumstances might trigger your resistance. Fatigue? Woundedness? When you don't feel safe? When life seems unfair? Pinpoint what might be holding you back from both receiving and giving love in your life.

2. Name someone who is hard for you to love. Can you recognize what is hard to love about this individual? What do you think God sees when He looks at this person? Does God choose, commit, and practice this committed choice in His love for this person? How do you know this to be true?

3. Think about how you might be "working up your own love" for people rather than allowing Jesus to love them through you. What does such effort produce in you? How

can you shift the source of your love from yourself to God by letting Jesus love people through you?

4. Memorize 1 Corinthians 13:4–8. Meditate on each phrase— one each day of the week—and ask God to grow this facet of love in your life.

Dear Jesus, I find it hard to love some people in my life. Help me to see them the way You see them and to love them the way You love them. In Your name, Amen.

> **"We love because he first loved us." (1 John 4:19)**

The fruit of Love looks like . . .

- Accepting your children and grandchildren no matter what they've done or said. (Gail)
- Showing mercy and compassion even when undeserved. (Caryl)
- Seeing as Jesus sees. (Toni)
- Caring for the elderly through the Meals on Wheels program. (Allison)
- Sticking with and growing through difficulties with people I am in relationship with to better understand each other and grow closer to each other. (Christy)

- Forgiving my ex-husband. (Iris)
- My husband humbly cleaning the bathroom and never saying a word about it. (Barbara)
- Compassion for others. (Robin)

CHAPTER 5

Joy

Confidence in God

Cherry. *In one juicy and tangy bite, the cherry offers its splendor. But watch out! Before swallowing its delicious meat, the pit must be discarded.*

Many of us think of joy as happiness. But joy and happiness differ, don't they?

Happiness comes from the root *hap*, which means "chance." Happiness is circumstantial. It has to do with life going the way we want it to go and the feeling we experience when that happens— like a Christmas morning where your favorite relatives are present, cooperate with your schedule, and genuinely like their gifts. Like a peaceful winter evening with kids snuggled up on the couch, the pooch too, and contentedness settled over the room. Like a perfect wedding day where the sun shines, the flower girls behave, and family and friends get along. Like the arrival of a robust and healthy baby, carefully placed on its mother's chest and welcomed.

Happiness. It's a good feeling based on good circumstances. No doubt, happiness is something to enjoy and celebrate on those occasions when it *happens*. Indeed, in these times, legitimate and pure joy bubbles up and overflows from our hearts.

But there are so very many other moments when life doesn't *happen* according to our desires! What then? What can we expect when life turns upside down, when we get nothing we want and everything we don't want?

Ah! That's also an opportunity for joy. Because where happiness is circumstantial, joy is not. Joy is more than happiness. It appears in both the great and the not-so-great moments of life because it is not dependent on circumstances.

The Old Testament describes joy as a quality of life as well as an emotion. The spontaneous songs of worship contained in the Psalms illustrate this kind of joy. Joy is a deep quality that celebrates God's character despite the conditions. Shouts of joy—after a costly battle (Psalm 20:5). Joy that comes in the morning—following a night of mourning (30:5). Garments of joy—that replace sackcloth (30:11). Songs of joy— that celebrate God's faithfulness (132:9).

In the New Testament, joy is often expressed as ecstasy, a feeling of amazement, an uninhibited response to God's grace and presence in our days—like the tidings of joy brought to the shepherds by the angels at the birth of Christ (Luke 2:10). Jesus connects joy with love in His parting words to His disciples in John 15:9–12. Paul declares that followers of Christ *are* his joy in Philippians 4:1.

New Testament writers, looking toward heaven and the resolution of their anguish, also connect joy to hope, love, and a perspective that sees beyond the immediate to the eventual. The writer of Hebrews depicts Jesus enduring the pain of the cross because of "the joy set before him" (12:2), and James challenges his readers to "consider it pure joy" when encountering trials (1:2).

When all the roots are uncovered and all the meanings parsed and defined, the Bible offers an overall definition of this elusive quality. To be honest, it surprises me. The fruit of joy is our heart's expression of confidence in God. Joy roots in, and ripens irrepressibly from, our complete faith in God's character—despite circumstances, despite what *happens*, despite the "pitty" moments in life that threaten to steal our joy.

One commentator concludes, "Joy is not just preliminary joy. It is a reference to the future experienced as joy in the present."[1] Joy is the ability to hold up because we know we are being held up. Joy is the conviction that God is in control of every detail of our lives, even when those details slip beyond our control. Odd though it might seem, when we understand the real fruit of joy, we can embrace Ron Rolheiser's suggestion that "joy and pain are born at the same place within us."[2]

Many of my readers have expressed this to be true as well. Allison reports that joy is "remaining positive when the circumstances in my life look hopeless or dire." Jill says joy is "contentedness in the midst of circumstances I'd rather not be in." And Barb says, "Joy is that wonderful feeling deep inside that everything's going to be okay no matter what the world around me looks like."

Holly finds a deep thread of joy throughout her life story: "I am a thirty-nine-year-old, broke single gal who lives with a couple of roommates, friends I went to school with. Especially in recent years I have struggled on and off with the longing to be a mother and the fear that the opportunity is slipping away from me. One thing that has been of great encouragement to me is remembering that my most important, primary identity isn't that of my parental status (mother or non-mother). Instead, my primary identity is that I am a Christian, that I am a child of God, a daughter of the King. And He has made me the way I am, with the personality and heart I have, for a reason (a heart that is tender and nurturing). So, I can seek Him and ask Him to reveal to me how He wants to use me and why He designed me the way He did, even if I don't bear the official 'title' of Mother (at least to the world). And that brings me joy, but it also allows me to reflect His joy even when I feel as if my life isn't going the way I maybe was expecting it to, the way I was planning to write it."

Similarly, Betsy lays out her lifetime of experiencing the fruit of joy. "Having severe Lupus for the last thirty-eight years and much organ damage, happy-face joy is not what I have. I am sixty-two now. Thankfully, God allowed me to raise my sons. Their dad could not handle me not being perfect, thus divorce and a custody battle. Now years later, I have a deep abiding joy knowing that God has been so faithful in all situations. He has never left a need unmet!!! That to me is deep abiding joy!"

Joy is confidence in God.

Joy comes on a Christmas morning spent with unfavorite relatives who show up late and with whiny children who gripe about their gifts. It boldly turns its gaze to the reason behind the celebration—God's gift of grace in Jesus—and remembering this, joy inhales with deep confidence.

Joy arrives in the winter turned blizzardly. When families hole up in small spaces for longer than they'd like . . . when emotions erupt and tempers shorten to match the ebbing daylight . . . joy shows up. It discovers forgotten board games and new playing skills in family members. And it reclaims the seemingly lost appreciation of one another.

Joy reaches into a rainy wedding day with grumpy flower girls who stubbornly plop down in mid-aisle, refusing to budge, forcing the bride to pick her way around the pile of toile to reach her groom. Fueled by a love that recognizes "in sickness and in health, in wealth and in poverty," joy welcomes the "whatever" of this sacred celebration.

Joy rises up out of cascading fear when a baby doesn't breathe in the first moments after delivery. With eyes searching a spouse for hope and hands reaching out for proof of life, joy swallows terror and resolves that this little life is being held by hands bigger and more capable than those of a mere mother, father, or even a doctor.

Joy is confidence in God no matter what *happens*. Because we've become convinced that God's character can be trusted always, we can be joyful in all life's moments—good, bad, confusing, sorrowful, challenging, unfathomable. Our understanding wraps us up and holds us in place. We know that just as God has come through before, He will come through again.

Joy has a way of buoying us up in the midst of the unpredictable. We're somehow hopeful. Strong. Clear. Confident. No, not la-la-lobotomized. We still wonder. We still worry. We still cry and fear and yearn. But beneath all our feelings is the conviction that we, and all that we care for, rest in the hands of an unchanging God who is in control. No matter what.

When we are young in life, or in our faith, it may be hard to fathom how we can absorb such a concept of joy. We've tasted only lightly of life's terrors. We are mothers who still idealistically believe we can stand between disappointment and our daughter, between tragedy and our son. We are people bent on creating a safe world for those we love, a cocoon of predictable provision. We are workers determined to climb the ladder, spouses assured we will stay married, grown children confident we can care for our elderly parents while mothering, working, and doing life without missing a beat.

Perhaps in these seasons we can't completely embrace this full-orbed joy. But by taking small steps toward joy in our early days, maybe we can develop a recognition of this fruit and our need for it as life's steps steepen.

When I discovered that my fourth-grade daughter had a learning disability, joy was the reassurance that God already knew this, and He knew what it would mean for her.

When I was told that my mother had cancer, joy was the security that the days of her life were numbered before I even came to be.

When my husband was suddenly hospitalized with a life-threatening blood infection while I was speaking—continents away—joy blanketed me as I served in place, prayed for him, and made emergency arrangements to return.

When my brother discovered he needed a liver transplant, and he had only me to serve as his chief caregiver while living thousands of miles away, joy arrived through the team of friends and family who committed to help in a myriad of ways, and through my own willingness to receive their help.

Today, realizing there are moments when I can't protect my children, and now my grandchildren, from all the dangers of this world, joy is the security that God is present in their lives always, even when I am absent. They will walk where I cannot go. But God is already there.

I don't want to pop the bubble of hope provided by youth, newness in the faith, or even denial. But I do know, from falling myself and being caught in the grasp of a God I can't escape, that life is unpredictable and contains many unpleasant moments. When such moments occur, we experience what it means to hold on because *we know that we know that we know* that we ourselves are being held. And in that confidence grows the full fruit of joy. And joy is a big, juicy mouthful of nourishment—even when it comes with a pit that will need to be discarded.

Joy is a surprising fruit. It's not the nice version of life we thought we signed up for. It's not about getting what we want when we want it. It's about God and His character—and what we really believe about Him. Such joy is way more than the happiness that *happens* when life *happens* to go the way we want.

Yes, joy is confidence in God. It's a cherry—a sweet treat despite the pit in the middle.

Joy reveals to us what we believe about God. Further, it reveals what we believe about God to those who watch and wonder how we'll respond when life *happens* to let us down.

Get Growing

1. When we observe joy in others—when we see a solid confidence in God's character that the normal and even sensational bumps of life can't alter—we are impressed. We find ourselves drawn to know the God who can produce such a state in mere mortals. Think about your family and friends. Who exhibits the kind of joy we've been talking about in this chapter? How does their example shape your heart?

2. The philosopher Nietzsche once said about believers in Jesus, "I would believe in their salvation if they looked a little more like people who have been saved." Do you look like you've been "saved"? What would joy look like in your personality? In your particular circumstances today?

3. A few generations ago, there was a popular acronym for joy that went:

   J: Jesus First

   O: Others Second

   Y: Yourself Last

   What do you think of such a definition and ordering? What could be helpful from this mantra as you live a life of joy and as you teach your children to do so? What might be the inherent dangers of such an attitude?

4. Read Philippians 4:4 where Paul challenges his readers to "rejoice in the Lord." What does it mean to put the word *joy*, a noun, into a verb form? How do we *do* joy? Or how do we "joy" in our lives?

Dear Jesus, real joy is a bit scary. It's facing the good and the bad of life—with You, knowing that You are God over all. Help me to courageously put my confidence in You today, so that no matter what happens tomorrow, I will be able to experience the joy of knowing You are in control of both. In Your name, Amen.

> **"Consider it pure joy, my brothers and sisters, whenever you face trials of many kinds." (James 1:2)**

The fruit of Joy looks like . . .

- My joy in the ordinary moments of life has increased since accepting God's forgiveness and love! (Lisa)
- Joy is not carefree, blindly going through the day. It is the WAY I move through my day, choosing to focus on the positive, living in gratitude for all I have been given,

acknowledging God's movement in situations and in answered prayers. Joy is also found in looking for the good in others. There is contentment in a life full of Joy. (Cindy)

- I keep my eyes open for things little and big that spark joy. That mindset makes it easier to sense when my focus switches to worry and joy seems to slip away. (Glenda)
- Joy is knowing absolutely that God has me. (Iris)
- Being able to dance and sing again after my firstborn son died. (Stacy)
- Music is how I express joy. I love to sing about Jesus's love for me and others. I love to praise Him in worship during a church service. There is always a song in my heart and in my head. (Ann)
- Joy is that gut-level emotion that exceeds happiness. I find joy in my everyday life as a chaplain. It brings me great joy when I am able to sing a hymn to someone with dementia who can remember every word. (Diane)
- Knowing that God sees me, knows me, and cares, even in the midst of circumstances that are difficult. (Ann)

CHAPTER 6

Peace

Resting in God

Blueberry. *The blueberry is heart healthy, providing the largest fruit source of antioxidants that prevent cancer and other diseases. It also possesses anti-aging and anti-infection properties. Blueberries reduce the results of stress in our lives.*

Typically we think of peace as the absence of irritation. A quiet afternoon of naptime for the kids and, for us, a cup of coffee with a good read. No phone calls. No demands on our time and attention.

The fruit of peace listed in Galatians 5 conveys something different. In the original New Testament Greek, "'peace' in the sense of 'freedom from worry' . . . was often expressed by means of an idiom, for example, 'to sit down in the heart,' 'to rest in the liver,' or 'to be quiet in one's inner self.'"[1]

There is a story about a king who offered a prize to the artist who would paint the most compelling picture of peace. Hundreds of entries poured in, many depicting a somewhat stereotypical view of tranquility. Beach scenes at sunset. Mountain streams. Wide valleys framed by hills where sheep grazed in safety.

The king surprised participants and his court with his selection. Rather than choosing the best of the best of these tranquil portrayals, he decreed an unusual painting to be the most accurate expression of peace.

The artist depicted a raging storm—wild and tumultuous. Imagine yourself in that painting, standing before the whirl, wet spray blowing across your cheeks. Thunder rumbles in your bones, reverberating through your body. Before you lies an open field, in the middle of which a solitary tree stands against the howling wind, bowed by its strength. And tucked into one of the branches is a nest where a mother bird cups her babies in safety. She has built a place of rest for herself and her family. In it she hides, secure and calm amidst the gale.

A one-word title captured the painting's offering: *Peace*.[2]

Mark 4:35–41 describes a scene much like this painting. The disciples were on the Sea of Galilee, with Jesus in the boat asleep, when a wild storm came up. As the waves broke over the boat, threatening to sink it, they cried in terror to their sleeping teacher, "Don't you care if we drown?" Jesus got up, rebuked the wind and the waves, then questioned the disciples about their lack of faith. Did they have none?

Peace is the result of resting in God. Peace comes from resting in a relationship that holds us in the midst of life's storms—as well as in the momentary calm of their aftermath.

Sleeping through the storm, Jesus exemplified the true meaning of peace that arises from rest. Jesus rested in the boat—in the storm—because He rested in His relationship with His Father. Completely convinced of God's control over the externals, Jesus could relax to the point of sleep.

Rest? How does that work for us in our everyday lives? To most of us, rest is a four-letter word—an impossibility we take on our tongue and then spit out in frustration when we don't get it. We race from carpool to dentist to meeting to market. Beckoned by the washer, needy children, and the weekend's activities, we march according to the orders of others. Rest? When? How? It's funny how a good thing like rest can send us into a tailspin of effort. It feels so all up to us to manufacture, doesn't it? If we had more faith, more patience, more laid-back-ness, wouldn't we be more restful and therefore more peaceful?

Silly us! We attack the subject of rest with an itinerary that spells DO IT! and end up undoing the very result we're after.

The Chinese pictograph for *busy* is made up of two characters: *heart* and *killing*. Busyness kills our hearts. Rest restores our souls. The spiritual fruit of peace comes when we wash away the killing and focus instead on the heart of living. That means our relationship with God.

Author Henry Blackaby tells of his visit to a farmer on his land. He called ahead for directions and received a blurry commentary containing the exact number of fence posts, certain colors of silos, and the lay of ditches he must follow. Henry carefully followed the instructions and made it to the farm, but tension and anxiety accompanied him throughout the journey.

His next trip to the farm was different. Henry felt easy, relaxed, and peaceful, and not just because it was his second time around. This time the farmer was his passenger. Henry merely had to take directions—"Turn right at the silo . . . now keep it at no more than thirty because it's bumpy . . . okay, up ahead at that stand of trees, we'll veer left"—and he arrived safely. Resting in his relationship with his friend, Henry experienced peace as he drove.

When we experience God's presence, peace results. Gayle muses, "I have inner peace that even though our income is being cut in half with me exiting my employment, God will provide. His peace passes every ounce of understanding I think I have." Dawn testifies, "When we lost our twenty-year-old son, I knew God was carrying me along that dark hard path." When Lisa struggles with anxiety over tight schedules, money, and her children, she takes a deep breath and tries to give it all to God. She shares, "Almost always I feel my anxiety lessen and am able to get through the moment and feel at peace knowing I am not alone." Elizabeth says, "Peace was hard to come by after being rejected by my husband and with my body betraying me with illness. God has shown me in time that what He feels about me is so much more important than anything else. I had to let go of things that held me back from having His peace."

In Matthew 11:28–30, Jesus calls us to His rest that produces peace. "Come to me, all you who are weary and burdened, and I will give you rest. Take my yoke upon you and learn from me, for I am gentle and humble in heart, and you will find rest for your souls. For my yoke is easy and my burden is light." Earlier, in verse 27, we find the clue as to why rest is possible: "All things have been committed to me by my Father. No one knows the Son except the Father, and no one knows the Father except the Son and those to whom the Son chooses to reveal him." Jesus invites us to join in the rest He Himself enjoys with the Father.

Colleen shared a story of the peace she experienced when God revealed His tender presence. "On my way to work one morning, I was praying over our family during a time of divorce. As I approached the red light and stopped, right in the middle of the intersection were two doves. They stayed there the entire time, and I sensed God saying, 'There is peace in your crossroads.' My heart flooded with peace. As the light turned green, I slowly entered the intersection, anticipating the doves would fly away. They stayed until I was through it, and in my rearview mirror, they were still there. . . . I sensed the Lord saying, 'Peace, be still.' Since that day, peace (for the most part) has helped guide me through this season."

Years ago, as I was boarding a flight to return from Washington, DC, to Denver, my phone buzzed. I learned that my daughter, twenty weeks pregnant, was losing her son. The thought of sitting trapped in a steel tube for over three hours, as she labored and her husband supported her, seemed incomprehensible. But as the plane's doors closed, I imagined God's hands guiding my flight across the sky, holding me tightly in His embrace and preparing me as I rested in His peace. Then I realized He was also holding the hand of my daughter, her husband, and my older grandson. When I landed, I zoomed in warp speed to my daughter's side, but the hours of restful peace had strengthened me. Oh, there were still painful moments as our dear little Malachi slipped from this world—many of them! But God's peace carried us, and it still does.

Both in such big moments and in our daily struggles, we can experience deep anxiety—even though we know better (or think we do). It's okay. God will not leave us alone. God will provide for our needs. God will be present with us in our fears. He longs for us to have the healthy life that is only possible when we experience His peace—the stress-relieving "blueberry" fruit of the Spirit that comes from resting in Him.

How do you, like a little bird in a howling storm, need to build a nest of rest in a relationship? Where can you simply lay down the busyness and meet life with a more openhanded stance that receives whatever it brings you? Peace can come anytime. In the middle of the night with a sick child. During the day, when the dog and the phone and your teen all ring out their needs around you. While you're caught up late in a meeting and can't go where you need to when you need to be there. Peace can come in all these circumstances because peace flows from our relationship with the God who is with us in such stormy moments.

Life's irritations come and go. Harsh, painful circumstances are inevitable. That at-ease moment when irritations are absent is nice, but that's not the fruit of peace. Rather, the "blueberry" fruit of the Spirit embraces the calm that comes from resting in God in even the hardest times.

Get Growing

1. Still not sure what it might look like to find peace resulting from rest in real life? Amid the daily bustle, when anxiety seems overbearing, sit down and take several long breaths as you listen to God beckoning you: "Come to me, my weary, burdened child, and I will give you rest." In the most everyday moments, you can "practice the presence" of God like this. Peace is the result of resting in a relationship with a real God who is really there.

2. Stereotypes of peace can get in the way of experiencing the real thing. Make a mental list of the ideas you carry that *seem* like peace to you but which, upon inspection, prove to be a wrong belief about peace.

3. Read Mark 4:35–41. Put yourself in the place of both the disciples and Jesus. What emotions do you experience? Why? What can you learn from the disciples' response? And from Jesus'?

4. What do you think peace means to children? When they watch the news and see horrendous things happening, how

can your new understanding of this fruit help them handle what they see?

Dear Jesus, I have to admit that peace has always seemed so . . . well, nice to me. I've often viewed it as the absence of hassle and hard things in life—and therefore something beyond my control. Help me apply the understanding that peace is the result of resting in a relationship with You in the midst of irritation, not just in the absence of it. When I'm bugged, help me seek Your presence to process what I'm feeling. In Your name, Amen.

"Peace I leave with you; my peace I give you. I do not give to you as the world gives. Do not let your hearts be troubled and do not be afraid." (John 14:27)

The fruit of Peace looks like . . .

- The deep-down calm and happiness that comes from knowing and walking with Jesus and feeling safe in His hands. (Robin)

- A deep tranquility, even in troubling circumstances, knowing that God has brought me through before. He will not leave me nor forsake me. My mind rests. (Nell)

- The presence of Christ in and around me when the world is falling apart. (Lonni)
- Knowing God is in control. (Karen)
- A quiet in my heart even though the world is swirling around me. (Jill)
- Resting in Him, knowing I am under His wings, in His hands, and loved. (Jan)
- A sense of harmony with God. Even when things are far (oh so far) from tranquil, I can rest. I can breathe, even when I'm being squeezed, because God's got me. (Alexandra)

CHAPTER 7

Patience

Hanging In with People and Their Problems

Coconut. *A coconut is undoubtedly the toughest of all fruits. Its stonelike shell wards off all but the most damaging outer attacks, protecting the sweet meat within.*

Hurry up and wait. To most of us, patience is what we need when our schedules don't match up with life.

Usually, we think of patience as perseverance in trying circumstances. Racing to the doctor's office only to be told she's running late. Selecting the express lane at the market and then noticing the customer in front of us has way exceeded the fourteen-item limit. Having our return flight from a business trip canceled due to bad weather. Missing a school performance because of a traffic snarl. There's a very real kind of patience that has to do with such quandaries: patience with situations.

But the kind of patience addressed in the Bible's fruit list—sometimes translated "forbearance" or "longsuffering"—actually means patience with people. It is modeled after God's patience with humankind, as Peter writes: "He is patient with you, not wanting anyone to perish, but everyone to come to repentance" (2 Peter 3:9). God waits for us to want Him and His help. God suffers long with us out of His desire that we'll see our need for Him. God's patience illustrates the patience we need if we want to look like Him. The fruit of patience is patience with people—and their problems.

Uh-oh.

This kind of patience is about . . .

> . . . holding your hands back while your five-year-old creates her fifty-third pair of bunny ears to loop (whoops—missed it again!) into a shoelace bow, all the while puffing, "I can do it by myself!"
>
> . . . swallowing irritation when your girlfriend cancels lunch—again—because she has to take care of her sick child.
>
> . . . listening—a looooonnnnnnggggg time on the phone—to your lonely mom, who drones on and on and on about her life but shows little interest in yours.

Patience is hanging in with people and their problems. Oh, did I mention—their problems usually affect us as well.

A friend of mine let me down once—big time. She promised to cover a commitment for me and then didn't. It hurt others. It hurt me. I looked carefully at my own responsibilities in the matter. Perhaps I shouldn't have delegated the job to her. Okay. But she'd committed to me. *She* messed up. *She* let me down. *She* blew it. And I felt like blaming her and telling the whole world it was *her* fault. Not mine.

About that same time, my then eleven-year-old son spilled orange decongestant on my cream-colored carpet. My first attempts at stain removal seemed to make it worse. The stain spread. But eventually, with enough water and rinsing and sopping, the orange lessened to peach and then to pink. Almost gone. Almost. Removing it completely would take work—the chemical kind. After four applications of spot remover, the stain was finally out, or at least you couldn't see it through the suds of the cleaner.

Mistakes stain. And stains take work to remove. They don't automatically pick themselves up off carpets and walk down faucet drains. I had to clean up after my son. And on a deeper level, my friend and I had to work at cleaning up the stain on our relationship.

Likewise, someone has to work to remove the stain of sin. And Someone did. Jesus has done the hardest part already. The work He did on the cross when He died to forgive all our sins is done. Now Jesus asks us to join His work. Our job is to receive His love and forgiveness and extend them to others.

Patience is hanging in with people and their problems . . . sometimes to the point of forgiveness, always to the point of love. Patience is like a coconut. It is undoubtedly the toughest of all the fruits of the Spirit. Its stonelike shell defends against all but the most damaging of outer attacks and protects the sweet meat within. No wonder this fruit is so hard to practice in the raw day-to-day of life!

Responders to my survey for this book revealed that patience is one of the three hardest-to-grow fruits (next to joy and self-control). Cindy confesses that patience is hard for her because she's a "get things done kinda gal." She observes, "My timetable for repair and restoration is not always God's." Bethany is helped when she remembers that God is always patient with her. Iris shares her tip,

"I try to take a breath and stay still with my mouth shut." And Jessica admits, "Jesus has to help me every few hours with this one."

Likely we all relate to Carol, who writes, "Patience is the ability to wait for God to be about His work and His timing, trusting that He keeps His word. This is hard because we want to step in and control."

I so get this. I can become impatient with my loved one's dementia. I have to repeat my questions, slow down my accomplishments, and remember over and over again that this isn't something that can be changed. I struggle with the unpredictability of someone else I want to trust but can't when I sense that person has been drinking after promising to no longer do so. My heart hurts. And I long to move past another's overspending, but when I see it affect that person's family, I can't seem to move forward. I'm tempted to bail the person out, but I know I can't fix the problem.

Such people and their problems affect me and my life.

Our natural response when other people's problems affect us is hurt and anger and sometimes defensiveness. Patience doesn't mean slapping on a "nice" face and ignoring the reality of how we feel. When there's a bright orange stain in the middle of our cream-colored carpet, we can walk around it or cover it with a throw rug, but it's still there. Living as if it isn't won't do much for us or those around us.

Responses of pain and hurt need to be processed and experienced because we are, by nature, emotional beings. To deny such feelings is to deny who we are. But there is a way in which experiencing the hurt and anger and disappointment of offenses can lead to forgiveness. When we process our response to being wronged with God, the fruit of patience can grow from the tangled vines of our hurt.

This kind of patience, like all spiritual fruit, requires that we ask for it and cooperate with God in its growth in our relationships. We have to want Him to grow it in us. We have to let Him grow it in us. But patience seems to be one of the tougher fruits to grow. As with me with my friend, blaming and grudge bearing are so much more tempting.

What does it look like to cooperate with God in cultivating patience? Sometimes patience might look like saying a prayer for the person who has let us down. At other moments, patience will direct us to lovingly confront the one who has offended us. Or we might be pushed to love someone who's very hard to love because of how their problems have wounded us. On still other occasions, we will find patience leading us to forgive a person altogether for their bumbling blooper. And there are rare times when patience looks like creating space between us and people with problems because space is necessary for healing to occur.

Patience is hanging in and staying with people and their problems. Friends. Husbands. Children, for sure. Parents. Bosses. Neighbors. Coworkers. Pastors. Moms who parent differently. Competitive siblings. Judgy believers. Friends who let us down and sons who spill orange medicine.

Patience is more than a nice face we put on in a not-so-nice moment. It's a supernatural fruit that grows in the soil of our humanity. As we experience unwelcome wounds from people with problems, God can grow His fruit in our hearts and empower us to respond to real-life hurts with patience.

Get Growing

1. Review the difference between patience with circumstances and patience with people and their problems. What skills are necessary to deal with both? What skills are uniquely important for dealing with people and their problems?

2. Time to get down to it. Are you holding on to a grudge, stuck in unforgiveness, or unable to move toward a person who's wounded you or someone you love? Ask God to grow the fruit of patience in you for this specific relationship. Be honest about your emotions, as they need to be processed. Process what steps you might need to take to demonstrate patience in this spot in your life.

3. On the other hand, is there someone who needs patience with *you* because of a wound you've inflicted? What steps might you take to heal the matter from your end?

4. Read 2 Peter 3:9. How does the fact that God is unendingly patient with you impact your ability to be patient with others?

Dear Jesus, I'm thinking of _____. You know the situation. You were there. I feel _____ and _____ every time I remember this matter. Please help me release these emotions to You. They are real and I know it. Now, God, give me insight into how patience might look in the situation. Help me have the courage to demonstrate it, starting today. In Your name, Amen.

"Be patient, bearing with one another in love."
(Ephesians 4:2)

The fruit of Patience looks like . . .

- Telling the cashier-in-training at the store to take her time, and meaning it. (Allison)
- Answering my daughter's calls even if I have talked with her five times that day. Listening to her share her workday with me even if it's the same thing I heard yesterday. (Ann)
- Being long-tempered instead of short-tempered. (Barbara)
- Responding, not reacting. (Karen)
- Being able to show love and respect even when others are difficult to deal with. (Liz)
- Giving people the benefit of the doubt. (Gayle)
- Taking a lot of deep breaths and trying to listen well. (Janet)
- Stopping what I'm doing and paying attention to my husband recounting something he has read or learned. (Judy)
- Being slow to criticize or complain. (Robin)

CHAPTER 8

Kindness

Compassion in Action

Pineapple. *The pineapple has long stood as a symbol of hospitality. From Hawaii to New York, a pineapple as a gift welcomes guests to a home and underlines their inclusion in a family's circle.*

If there's one fruit that seems at first glance to fit the concept of "nice," it's kindness. To some of us, kindness conveys a charitable offering of help for the impoverished, economically challenged, or simply less fortunate. While kindness may well include extending care to those who have little in life, it does not demand a formulaic offering of niceness. And the needy are not the only folks in our lives who benefit from the fruit of kindness.

At its root, to be kind means to be useful. Kindness is compassion expressed in action. The Greek word for kindness used in the list of fruits in Galatians 5:22 means, "To provide something beneficial for someone as an act of kindness, 'to act kindly, to be kind, kindness.'"[1]

Let's take apart this definition a bit. First, kindness cares. It sees through the façade of a newly widowed friend who says she's "fine." It notices the woman in the line ahead who doesn't have quite enough cash to pay for her groceries. It senses the nervousness of a child who's been left in the church nursery for the first time.

Next, the compassion of kindness translates into action. After the death of Saul, King David inquired about any of Saul's remaining relatives to whom he could show God's kindness (2 Samuel 9:3)—a remarkable gesture since a new dynasty traditionally did away with all members of the prior one. A crippled son of Jonathan was brought forth, and David invited him to dine at the king's table "like one of the king's sons" (v. 11).

Kindness gets involved. It stops what it's doing and asks that widow friend to grab coffee. It catches the eye of the grocery clerk and offers a twenty for the woman ahead in line. It bends down low to ask the name of the new child at church.

When Judy was diagnosed with cancer, she made it her goal to bless the people she came in contact with during the process. Doctors, nurses, radiation techs, and other patients were often surprised by her uplifting words, her thanks and encouragement. She says, "I have continued to practice kindness to this day."

Kindness notices when an elderly neighbor hasn't been out and about for a few days, and it knocks on her door and checks on her health. Kindness anguishes over the HIV/AIDS crisis in Africa and sponsors an HIV-positive orphan, faithfully sending a support check each month. Because kindness cares that a husband is stressed and late, it rinses his dishes, takes the dog out for him, and stuffs in an extra load of wash. The compassion of kindness trickles over into pure, clean action—the kind that usually costs us something in terms of time and energy.

Carla shares an understanding of kindness that meets this perspective. "I think a root of kindness is noticing other people's needs. If we're just focused on ourselves, we don't see ways to be kind."

Cindy unpacks this approach further. "Kindness really is a heart to respond to a person, giving what they need in that moment, meeting them where they are to show them that they have a value and are worth the attention that I am giving them."

She continues, "Compassion is also a part of kindness. If I see that a person is struggling or hurting, I go to them and offer a hug of comfort or sit with them while they process a heartache. Kindness is helping a young mom with a toddler and a baby as she struggles to put her packages in her car after a trip to the store. Kindness is telling a stranger that they have toilet paper hanging out of the waistband of their pants. Kindness is doing for others what you would hope someone would do for you if the situation were reversed. Kindness is also looking for an opportunity to give an encouraging word."

As noted, the pineapple has long stood as a symbol of hospitality. Kindness is meeting needs; it's compassion expressed in action.

Maybe we can muster up such a response for the once-a-year clothing drive for the homeless. Or we can provide school supplies for inner-city kids, or take a meal to a new mom. All because we really do care and really do want to help. But sometimes kindness seems more costly than we can afford—like when we can't control the way someone will respond.

Colleen reveals, "As I've become older and wiser (I hope), I am realizing that being kind takes on a different role depending on who the receiver is. Some are so grateful and express gratitude for my kindness. Others will use it selfishly to work to their own advantage. However, it is when kindness consistently flows from the heart's intent that truth arises . . . regardless of how people receive it."

Robin has struggled to offer kindness to a friend, saying that kindness sometimes is "doing the hard thing when the easy thing is—easier." She goes on, "The world is full of selfishness. I want to be different. I want someone to know by my actions how much I *love* God. Specifically, I've prayed for a friend who frazzles me enough that I quietly bow out of gatherings that might include her. Instead of group gatherings, I reach out to just her on occasion, send her a birthday note or a thinking-of-you text."

In its execution, kindness carries an element of self-sacrifice that puts the needs of others before our own.

Carla discovered this one day at the market. "When I went in the grocery store, there was a lady standing by the door with a full cart. She was asking one of the workers how long a taxi would take, because she had already called, and they seemed to be taking a while. Older people taking taxis is pretty normal at this particular store.

"When I finished shopping, she was still standing there, just inside because it was getting windy. I asked her if I could give her a ride. I didn't want her to be uncomfortable, so I told her my name and she said she was Carol. Anyway, I took her home.

"Why does it feel so odd to take a risk with a stranger? I'm glad I drove Carol home today. Perhaps someday I'll be the one needing a ride, but even if not, I always want to be willing to extend myself."

You know where kindness is the costliest? At home.

It's hard to express kindness to those we know well, and it's even more challenging to be constantly kind to those we know best. Behind the closed curtains of home, our charitable smiles fade, and our willingness to help out winds down with the wearying messes and needs and questions. We snarl at the guy we loved enough to marry. We turn churlish toward our beloved children. In the middle of a tirade about how no one ever takes their shoes or books or toys up the stairs (they are all piled on the sides, so they're near-to-impossible to pass), the phone rings. And we automatically adjust our tone from Monster Mom to Spiritual Sally—*"Hellllooooo?"*

We try. Truly, we do. But to tell the truth, we seem to do a better job at extending kindness beyond our families, outside our homes than inside.

I wonder why.

Of course, we're tired. More tired inside home than outside. Here the needs are never-ending. They don't stop at 5:00 or 8:00 or even 11:00. We can control the influences and interruptions coming from outside our home, or at least choose which ones we'll respond to. Inside . . . well, meeting needs is what we're there for, isn't it? We can't ignore texts or dinnertime or errands that need to be run when it comes to family. When a child is sick, who else but Mom will fetch a cold washcloth? When a husband hits a schedule bump, of course we'll be the one to pinch hit for him. When our elderly parent needs a ride to the doctor . . . and then a prescription . . . and then home to be set up in a chair with the remote and a meal . . . you bet we'll say yes. We might sigh a bit, but we do it.

A major truth for moms, dads, and anyone else who caregives is that we can't give to others what we don't have ourselves. Oh, we think we're being incredibly selfless and spiritually mature to give and give to others while ignoring our own needs. But are we?

Even Jesus didn't ignore His own needs 24/7. In his gospel, Mark tells us that after Jesus healed Peter's mother-in-law, the whole needy town gathered to see Him. Yet "early in the morning, while it was still dark, Jesus got up, left the house and went off to a solitary place, where he prayed" (Mark 1:35). Kindness to others begins with kindness to ourselves. Think of it this way: What if it's *less* kind to ignore ourselves, so that we're rundown grouches, and *more* kind to do enough self-care to change our attitude? What if that's what Jesus meant when He encouraged us all to love our neighbor as we love ourselves? What if receiving God's love and kindness toward ourselves is what it means to look like Jesus in this attribute of kindness? See, we can only be kind to others when we continue to replenish our tank of kindness by being kind to ourselves.

Let's bring this fruit home—literally. In order to be kind to those closest to us, we need to be kind to ourselves.

Kindness is compassion expressed in action. Kindness is getting up and meeting a need because it's there and we care.

Get Growing

1. Read the story of David's kindness in 2 Samuel 9. What strikes you about his action? Did Jonathan's son *deserve* kindness?

2. Do you try to give what you don't have? Go to the King of Kindness. When you're running on empty in your kindness tank, it helps to remember how kind God has been to you. Name five specific actions God has taken to demonstrate His kindness in your life.

3. Are you kind to yourself? After focusing on receiving God's kindness, practice kindness toward yourself. Make room in your day—or night—for an activity that meets *your* need. A bath. A cup of tea. A chapter in a book. Five minutes of quiet. It doesn't have to be a huge deal, but when you treat

yourself with an act of kindness, you'll be better able to do the same with others. What practice of kindness can you begin for *you*?

4. Determine to wake up with kindness. Turn around the myth that kindness is best expressed outside the home. Instead, start your kindness at home. Be intentionally kind to those you love the most, and watch how your actions and attitude multiply to those outside your walls. Which family member could use your kindness right now? What action could you take to demonstrate kindness today?

5. Open your eyes to the needs about you today. Whether in a simple or a more demanding way, watch for where God might be inviting you to invest.

Dear Jesus, I have to admit, I'm running on empty when it comes to kindness at home! There doesn't seem to be enough of me. But I know there is always enough of You. Please show me how to receive the kindness You have for me and how to be kind to myself—and then, out of that fullness, how to share kindness with those I love the most. In Your name, Amen.

"Be kind and compassionate to one another."
(Ephesians 4:32)

The fruit of Kindness looks like . . .

- Doing things for others, taking candy to work, running errands for those who are too busy, helping others to have a better day because of something I've done. (Amy)
- When I don't mind if someone cuts in front of me. . . . You never know what someone is going through! (Kathy)
- Smiling at someone I don't know who looks like they're having a difficult day. (Allison)
- Taking my pups over to see my elderly neighbor when I see him sitting out, because I know it will make him happy. (Stacy)
- Being gentle to people who are hurting with a gentle touch or a word of encouragement. (Iris)
- Holding the door open for someone. Driving at slower speeds so others can change lanes without having to force their way in. (Lisa)

CHAPTER 9

Goodness

Being like God Inside and Out

Strawberry. *The strawberry wears its seeds on the outside. With no apologies, this tangy fruit proclaims its nature, sharing its seeds as it grows.*

We use the word *good* loosely. We apply it to dogs, days, parties, children, job performance—to anything we measure. But in a spiritual sense, what is goodness?

The word *good* means excellence in character or constitution. In Galatians 5, it's connected to morality[1] and also to generosity.[2] When used as an exclamation, it's actually a substitute for God, as in, "Oh, goodness!"[3] Goodness is . . . well, perfection.

Great. How are we ever going to get that fruit growing in our lives?

Since the fruits of the Spirit are characteristics of God exhibited in our unique personalities, we can begin by understanding the goodness of God. Psalm 119 offers some clarity: "You [God] are good, and what you do is good" (v. 68). I like the simplicity of this verse, don't you?

God is good in His essence. His character is good. Ask any mom what she's teaching her child, and on the list will be something like "to be good." Goodness is not natural to us. We have to learn to be good. But goodness is totally natural to God. He *is* good. His very being is good.

God is also good in His actions. God does good things. His actions are always consistent with His character. When the Bible says that God is good, it means God acts in good ways in our lives for His good purposes. And just what is that purpose? To make us more like Him.

Maybe you remember a little prayer said as a child over a meal: "God is great. God is good. Lord, we thank you for this food." We know God is great. We believe He is good. But we stub our toe on doubt over the next question: Is God good to *me*?

Sometimes we know that we know that we know that God is good to me. Our precious children fill our heart with gladness. Money stretches to meet all our needs with a little extra for a meal out, a new outfit, and even that sofa we've been eyeing. God is good to give us what we need. When our lives are full and we have what we want, we enjoy His goodness. In such moments we think, "Yep—God is great. God is good. And. . . yep, He's good to me."

But in other times, we wonder, "*Is* God really good—to *me*?" Our child becomes ill, very ill. We lose our income. There's not enough money for any extras at all and barely enough for food and clothes. Life is challenging. Schoolchildren are gunned down. Miscarriage steals hope. Tornadoes take out whole towns. Parents become unable to care for themselves. Suffering overtakes our everyday. God doesn't seem good to me anymore.

What's happened? Between the "God is good to me" moments and the "Is God really good to me?" times, what changes? Well, it isn't God. The Bible teaches that God is the same yesterday, today, and tomorrow. He's either good when good things happen *and* when bad things happen or He's not good when *either* happens. What changes is our view of God. When times are good, we see God's goodness. When times are tough, we don't.

Perhaps it helps to tease apart the difference between kindness and goodness. At its root, kindness has to do with what a person does. Goodness concerns who a person is. We've defined kindness as compassion expressed in action. Goodness, on the other hand, sees the needs but doesn't necessarily purpose to meet them. Why? Because the goal of goodness is to make us like God. And meeting needs doesn't always accomplish such an objective.

Just as God is good to give us what makes us happy, He is happy to give us what makes us good. His actions consistently push us to the point where we will eventually resemble Him. Sometimes that means withholding what we think we want in order to provide what He knows we need. And God knows that we seem to grow more during the lean times than during the full times of life.

Wait—am I saying that God makes horrible stuff happen to us so we'll be more like Him? No. That's not what the Bible teaches. But God can and does use the hardest of times to help us grow. He won't waste them. He is as present in the unhappy, unfulfilled moments as He is in the fulfilling times. Romans 8:28 underlines this reality: "In all things God works for the good of those who love him, who have been called according to his purpose."

How does a good God grow such a good fruit in our lives? God begins the seed of this fruit on our insides—in our beings—and grows it outwards to our actions. Goodness is becoming like God in every respect in good and bad times alike.

I mused over this inside-out lesson about goodness years ago when my son was in about fifth grade. One afternoon he stomped in from play, steamed because his friend had excluded him from a game of street hockey. While I wanted to call the friend's mom and insist that her son include my little darling in his precious game, I held back and instead, worked with Ethan on his temper.

But the next morning, Ethan came to breakfast, still in a rotten mood. He grunted at me, refused to respond to my questions, and rolled his eyes at my directive that he rearrange his attitude. Hey—I'd fixed him, hadn't I? What was wrong with him? Why didn't he move past this spot? Now I was steamed.

Breakfast dishes were spread across the counter. Grabbing juice glasses and coffee cups, I shoved them into their wire partitions in the top rack of the dishwasher. The clock showed five minutes to the first school bell. And we were still here, in a mess. My anger grew. I threw the dishwasher door up, clanging it against the upper rack, which was still extended, and shoved rack, glasses, and cups into their place. The catch caught with a click, and I heard a slight tinkling sound from within.

Yikes. Carefully, I opened the dishwasher door. More tinkling sounds. Tentatively, I peered inside. Shards from what used to be three juice glasses hung at odd angles from the upper rack. As I lifted one cup, chipped but still intact, a concept in the Bible filtered into my thoughts. I remembered Jesus confronting the teachers of the law with their hypocrisy; they strove to ensure the outside of their lives looked good but never addressed the deeper issues of greed and selfishness within. Jesus told them, "First clean the inside of the cup and dish, and then the outside also will be clean" (Matthew 23:26).

Whoops. That's what I was doing with Ethan: merely fixing

his display of temper, nothing more. Focusing on the outside—making it look good—and forgetting about the inside. I'd wiped the surface of the situation clean but ignored what was really troubling my son and why. Why had he been angry? What were his expectations? What had he done with them? What needed to be processed and released? You know the drill. Perhaps too much for a fifth grader but not too much for his mom.

Looking good on the outside isn't what matters to God. God cares about our *being* good, the way He is good. So He gives us good opportunities for this fruit to grow. Goodness starts with who we are in our beings and works from the inside out—similar to how strawberries wear their seeds on the outside.

Left to ourselves, we're like those teachers in the Bible, preoccupied with the external. But when God comes in and housecleans the inside of who we are, forgiving our errors and making us clean internally, then we're good in every respect, both in our beings and in our actions. Goodness can't be clothed in superficiality and still be good. It's consistent from its inner core to its outer expression.

Cindy's words hit home. "A few years ago I would have said that goodness is related to being good, doing the right thing. I subconsciously held myself to a list of things I did to prove I was a 'good girl.' A lot of those were things I did *not* do. I realize now that likely I've lived much of my Christian life judging others by my 'goodness scale,' elevating myself in self-righteousness and looking down on others who didn't measure up in my opinion." Dawn shares, "Goodness is where the rubber meets the road. If I'm not living out what I'm professing, then I'm a hypocrite. Goodness is a by-product of an earnest abiding in Christ, where integrity, honesty, and a fruitful life are cultivated." And oh, how I love Ray's comment: "Only God is good, but I really want to be like Him."

God is good in His being and in His actions, in who He is and in what He does. The fruits of the Spirit are His characteristics evidenced in our personalities. We can't be good on the outside without God first making us good on the inside. But once this process begins, then through good times and bad, the fruit of goodness grows in us and we become more like God, inside and out.

Get Growing

1. What's the difference between inner and outer goodness? Think of this example: we might compliment a friend on her cooking, saying she's a good cook (action) without meaning she's a good woman (being). Similarly, a counterfeit twenty-dollar bill can accomplish much good (action) in the world without being good itself (being). How does this inside/outside distinction apply to you with your family, children, husband, neighbors, or coworkers? Are you good on the inside and not on the out, or vice versa?

2. C. S. Lewis holds that goodness isn't kindness because kindness simply wants to offer compassion in the face of suffering and doesn't care whether something is changed in the long run. Process the difference between kindness and goodness a bit. What is the goal of kindness? What is the goal of goodness? Why are both named as fruit of the Spirit?

3. Why do you think goodness is so important to God? Can you identify some spots where you resist God's fruit of goodness and why?

4. Memorize Romans 8:28. Now go further: make a list of the "all things" God is using in your life to work for good—on the inside and on the outside. How does this exercise change your thinking?

Dear Jesus, I have to admit that I'm not altogether comfortable with the fruit of goodness: being made like You inside and out. It seems so hard. But in the long run, goodness will grow in me. I know that. Please start with my inside to make me good. Clean me up and make me new. Then, I pray, grow this inner goodness into my outer actions. I also pray that I'd grow more and more in my desire for You to make both me and those around me good. I realize that might mean I may have to endure some struggles that don't look good to me. But I trust You to be good in Your being and Your actions, and I agree with Your purpose to make me good. In Your name, Amen.

> **"We know that in all things God works for the good of those who love him." (Romans 8:28)**

The fruit of Goodness looks like . . .

- Making sure my life matches what I say. (Ann)
- Having pure intentions toward others. (Becky)
- The general attitude of resembling my Father. (Bethany)
- Thoughtfulness on steroids. (Carol)
- Being honest with myself and others. (Iris)
- Integrity. (Jan)

- Any good that comes from me is from Jesus in me. (Joan)
- Doing what is right even if no one is watching. (Kristi)
- Remaining true to biblical commands and callings. (Robin)
- Returning a lost object to its rightful owner. (Steven)
- Choosing what God would choose. (Robin)
- God in us. (Lonnie)

CHAPTER 10

Faithfulness

Being True to God

Apple. *No fruit is more everyday than the apple. You can count on an apple as it is among the hardiest of fruits. Its easily identifiable form, red or green or gold skin, white pulp, and black seeds, labels it as the essential fruit for life. Its polished skin reflects its surroundings. An apple a day . . .*

We stood in church, my husband and I, voicing our way through worship songs. My ears heard the words. My spirit connected the theme: God's faithfulness. I mused over the concept as various phrases settled in my being. Great is Thy faithfulness. All my life You have been faithful. I'm standing on

Your faithfulness. He's faithful through all generations. Faithful You are, faithful forever You will be.

True words for sure. And yet my experience of God's faithfulness can ebb and flow depending on life's circumstances. When my house doesn't sell. When my friend's cancer doesn't respond to treatment. When I give in to temptation. Again. All after praying and praying and praying and trying desperately to trust God's faithfulness.

What exactly is the fruit of faithfulness?

When trying to define it, many readers jump straight to our faith in God, the way we love Him back for loving us. Diane says, "I have been steadfast in my faith." Dee shares, "My daughter has been dedicated to supporting the children's ministry at church for these past thirteen years. I have been faithful to my time with God every day." And Jill offers, "I remain faithful to God's calling in my life. To love Him and others as He continues to teach me how."

There's no doubt that our faith grows as our relationship with God grows. But is this kind of faith the same as the spiritual fruit of faithfulness? Is faith faithfulness?

Scripture says faith is a gift from God, a connection He creates in us. Paul famously writes, "It is by grace you have been saved, through faith—and this is not from yourselves, it is the gift of God— not by works, so that no one can boast" (Ephesians 2:8–9). Faith here is "to believe in the good news about Jesus Christ and to become a follower—'to be a believer, to be a Christian, Christian faith.'"[1] The idea is to possess strong confidence in and reliance upon someone or something; it has the sense of trusting. The same Greek word for faith is used in Hebrews 11, where the writer describes faith as "confidence in what we hope for and assurance about what we do not see" (v. 1). Faith is a vital and wonderful gift.

But it's different from the fruit of faithfulness.

In Galatians 5, we discover a different part of speech used to describe this concept. It's a slight but important tweak that shifts the focus from having trust in another person to being trustworthy ourselves. That's the fruit we're talking about: "trustworthiness, dependability, faithfulness"[2]—being someone who merits the complete confidence of others.

Faith is our response to a trustworthy entity, God. Faithfulness is the quality of being trustworthy ourselves, a person others can have faith in.

The spiritual fruit of faithfulness in us is an active response to God's faithfulness. As He keeps His promises to us, we reflect His faithfulness in how we live, both personally and in community. Like an apple's shiny skin, we mirror God's faithfulness by being true to Him and true to others.

True to God? How? God wants to spend time with us, so we spend time with Him. We can do this by reading the Bible, praying, and being part of a faith community in a church.

True to others? Yes. God wants us to be like Jesus in our relationships: dependable, loyal, committed, and true in our integrity and follow-through. This second, relational dimension is the arena where we can set in motion the faithfulness that grows through our times alone with God.

Faithfulness just may be the hardest of all fruits to understand. We get patience and kindness and love. But how do we wrap our arms around faithfulness? What does it mean to live it out in our everyday?

Several years ago, my husband and I moved from our larger family home into a townhome. Because we needed to make a quick decision when only a few homes were affordable options, we compromised on a home that lacked a main-floor primary bedroom and that had many (many!) stairs. And we made do, adjusting as needed. During Evan's recovery from shoulder surgery, he slept in the lowest level to avoid the tiring journey to his toothbrush. We stored our Christmas tree in the garage so we wouldn't have to drag it up another set of stairs. Daily we tromped upstairs and down while kidding each other that at least we were getting a workout. Meanwhile, our Jack Russell Terrier tried to figure out which floor we were on.

God has always provided "home" for us. From a tiny startup condo to the stair house, we've had a roof over our heads and walls that seemed to expand in various seasons to make room for our children and their children, for friends and other family members, and for umpteen cats and dogs. The stair house met our need at the time—but it was far from ideal. So, in great honesty and with a most-of-the-time yieldedness, I began praying pretty much right after we moved in that God would provide a more suitable situation. I knew He was faithful to provide, and I knew what I needed. So I asked for it.

Eventually, a much better home became available, and we prayerfully purchased it. But while we had swung a good deal, we still needed to sell the stair house. Guess what we heard from just about every potential buyer? "There are so many stairs!" "Oh, we just wish there was a main-floor primary bedroom!" Uh-huh. We found ourselves struggling with the decision we'd made.

Had we misheard God? Was He really providing, or had we overstepped?

I have to admit that there were many days in this process when I felt I was failing in this "trust trial." I often doubted and wibble-wobbled. God would remind me of all the other ways He'd been faithful in my past—with jobs and children and, yes, with homes. It took much more time than we desired for just the right family to walk through the door of our stair house and decide it was perfect for them. But eventually God provided and it sold.

Here's the thing: God is faithful. Whether or not He acts the way we want, when we want Him to, God is faithful. He is faithful to His character and to His good purposes for each of us. In 2 Timothy 2:13, Paul asserts, "If we are faithless, he remains faithful, for he cannot disown himself." He explains, "What if some were unfaithful? Will their unfaithfulness nullify God's faithfulness? Not at all!" (Romans 3:3–4).

Yes, God is faithful. No question here. The question is whether we will be faithful to Him. In slim seasons, or when we're suffering or challenged, or when His voice goes silent—or when the house doesn't sell—we can't produce faithfulness on our own. We have to turn to Him for the faithfulness we lack.

Help comes when we look to God's faithfulness as a model for how this fruit can look in our lives. Susan says, "I experience God's faithfulness daily. He wakes me and puts me to sleep. He answers my prayers. Great was His faithfulness in myriad ways as we recovered from a fire at our farm. He faithfully held me during breast cancer and sent friends and family to take care of us." Judy observes, "Faithfulness perseveres. It keeps on loving a difficult child even when the professionals suggest dumping them. It never gives up, even when it hurts. It continues to extend love to a parent who can no longer see, hear, or even remember you. When others desert, faithfulness continues to visit and draw near. Faithfulness consistently grows and nurtures a marriage decade after decade, through all the highs and lows, because a covenant has been made and faithfulness is a by-product of love."

When we bring our faith to God, we experience His faithfulness. Then we can mirror it to others. Dawn puts it this way: "God is constantly at work in this world and my life to make me more like my Savior. I see how He is faithful to fulfill His promises and is working to make sure I faithfully fulfill my promises to others." Robin agrees. "[Faithfulness involves] staying close to God and

His Word in our daily lives. As I go through the day, I can draw upon that presence and find ways to navigate and cope."

Think of faithfulness as looking into God's face, observing His unchanging trustworthiness, and then, by His Spirit, actually becoming an expression of His faithfulness. We mirror God's faithfulness to others, like Moses reflecting God's glory to Israel after spending weeks on the mountain with God, or like Jesus returning from His transfiguration to complete His Father's work on our behalf.

Faithfulness is being true to God, and by being true to Him, being true to others.

Get Growing

1. Have you ever experienced unfaithfulness in a relationship? Describe your emotions when someone was not true to you. How have you recovered from that experience? What lessons have you brought forward in life as a result?

2. On the other hand, name someone who has been faithful to you. What did such faithfulness feel like? How did it affect your life? How does such faithfulness motivate you to respond?

3. Consider a relationship that requires you to be faithful. How successful are you? What is the easiest part of being faithful to this person? What is the most challenging? How can you improve your faithfulness?

4. Is it possible to be 100 percent faithful to God and to others? Why or why not? How does your answer shape your efforts with this fruit?

5. Memorize 2 Timothy 2:13. In what moments have you experienced God's faithfulness in your own unfaithfulness? How do those examples impact your understanding of faithfulness?

Dear Jesus, I am in awe of Your faithfulness to me. To think that You are constantly available to me is beyond my comprehension. I don't think I've ever had such an offer in a human relationship. And yet there are so many times when I overlook Your faithfulness and ignore Your offer to be in a relationship. I'm sorry. Please help me to choose to be with You more often so I am acting upon my desire to be true to You. And please help me reflect Your faithfulness to me by being actively faithful to others You put in my life: my children, my parents, my husband, and my friends. May I be a mirror of Your faithfulness. In Your name, Amen.

> **"The Lord is faithful, and he will strengthen you and protect you from the evil one."**
> **(2 Thessalonians 3:3)**

The fruit of Faithfulness looks like . . .

- Dependability, in it for the long haul. (Barbara)
- Staying married for seventy years. (Beth)
- Trusting God, doing whatever He tells you to do. (Caryl)
- Remaining steadfast. (Kathy)
- Showing up with purpose. (Michelle)
- Total and complete reliance. (Donna)

- Keeping promises. (Karen)
- Through the Spirit's conviction over the years, true faithfulness follows. (Toni)
- Persevering and following God despite it all. (Jan)
- Clinging to God's faithfulness. (Michelle)

CHAPTER 11

Gentleness

Yielded to God's Desires

Banana. *The banana is a sensitive fruit. Its skin provides incomplete protection. If its skin is bruised, often so is the fruit within.*

We live in a world where those who wrestle their way to the top are esteemed. Gentleness is seen as wimpiness. Nobody wants to waste time being gentle when success is spelled T-O-U-G-H.

Many Bible authorities hold that the Greek word for gentleness in the Galatians 5 fruit list is the most difficult of all to translate into our language and culture. In contrast with dealing harshly with others, it conveys the idea of gentleness in attitude and behavior—of meekness, mildness, and endurance.[1] We picture soft-spoken personalities, mild-mannered interactions, and placidness, characteristics hard to square with being Jesus-like.

And yet, Jesus invites us to "take my yoke upon you and learn from me, for *I am gentle* and humble in heart, and you will find rest for your souls" (Matthew 11:29, emphasis added). What does gentleness mean here? Jesus is contrasting the burdensome requirements the Pharisees were laying out with the grace-filled obedience the Father invites. Jesus's gentleness involves receiving whatever yoke is required—"even death on a cross" (Philippians 2:8).

Perhaps the historical context can help us here. Centuries ago, the philosopher Aristotle described this word as the golden mean between extreme anger and extreme angerlessness. In ancient Greece, war horses were trained to be meek—strong and powerful and yet under control and willing to submit.[2] Gentleness is harnessed power. It is a submissive will. Picture an animal trained to reach its potential, then review Jesus's self-description in Matthew 11:29, and you'll see that gentleness is a soul yielded to God's desires.

Whoa. Now you're talking T-O-U-G-H.

There are sooo many moments in which to practice growing this fruit. I remember one—one summer way back in time, during the neighborhood prelims for the swim team championships. My daughter was a swimmer—an amazing talent, in my humble estimation. The top eight finishers from two heats would make it to finals. I felt confident.

I stood on the side, timer poised for the gun. Her dive was good. Straight off the block. Not too deep. She surfaced smoothly and began stroking. Quick, even strokes, slapping through the water. She came to the turn. A little slow . . . then she picked up speed again. Just a few more meters. She touched. Second in her heat. Good. After the next heat, I surmised she'd be third overall.

The finalists were posted. A mom came to tell me, "She made it!"

"Great!" I cheered. "What place was she?"

"Sixth," came her reply.

Out of my mouth came the words, "Only sixth? You're kidding! What happened?"

I looked down at my daughter. There she sat beside me, water dripping down her neck from under her cap, the flush of exertion still in her cheeks. My words echoed back to me. What more did I want? What was wrong with sixth? After all, places didn't matter in prelims. It was only necessary to make the top eight to qualify. And besides that, she was only nine years old in a neighborhood championship for nine-year-olds. What did I want?

I leaned down and whispered, "I just blew it, didn't I?" She nodded. I teared up and swallowed. "I'm sorry," I offered. She shrugged.

I've thought a lot about my response that day. Through the championships and in the years since, I've wondered about my gut reaction. What did I want? Did I want her to be a champion so she would have friends and acclaim? Did I want her to win so I'd be applauded? Did I want her to beat the whole lot just because it would be fun and she could do it?

Probably all of the above. But one day in the distant future, what difference would it make?

I think back to my poolside behavior and all the arrow prayers I had flung heavenward. Sure, I believed God cared about the details of my days and welcomed any and all of my concerns. But here I was, dragging my agenda around the lawn chairs, insisting on the fulfillment of my concept of best for my daughter.

It's a small example, but it represents a lifetime of growing the fruit of gentleness. Being yielded to God's desires means letting go of mine.

Friends, beware. Gentleness is a tricky fruit to grow because it requires surrender, and surrender makes us vulnerable. Oh baby, so very vulnerable. The banana is a sensitive fruit.

When we admit that we don't get to pick and choose what will or won't happen to our children, or whom they will or won't become, we recognize that what we invest in during their young days has an ending point. Eventually they will gather up the heap of stuff we've offered over the years, throw it in the trunks of their cars, and head off on their own. They might purpose to grow a life that matters—on their own initiative and terms—or they might not. But we don't get to choose. They do.

We don't get to control what our husbands choose: a better job with better pay or staying put in a loyal spot. Reconciling with his sister or avoiding her altogether. Growing with God or plateauing.

We don't get to choose how our parents will respond in their declining health. How our supervisors will evaluate and reward—or not reward—our performance. What things our neighbors include us in socially. Or even how our country decides to move into the next decade. We aren't in charge of oh, so very much.

I've got to admit, I don't like this part of life. It's hard to let go of command-central of my own days. You mean God knows what's better for me and who I want to become than I do? No way!

Yes way.

Susan discovered God's gentleness in "His Holy Spirit whispering to me during a stressful week leading up to my daughter's wedding at our farm." Michele offers that gentleness is "approaching difficult situations with grace and love, though sometimes through gritted teeth." Amy muses over her need for patience as she's helping her son with fifth grade math homework. "His meltdowns over not understanding the material require me to be very gentle with him." Robin sums it up, "I surrendered all that I am to God some time ago, and in doing that, I felt more protected and safer than ever."

We may not be in charge, but we are able to yield—in how we parent, how we express love in marriage, what our work life looks like, how we care for our aging parents, and how we live out our influence in this world. We are able to offer the fruit of gentleness in a way that honors our good God and His perfect desires.

In her book *A Faith That Will Not Fail*, Michele Cushatt offers this perspective on gentleness: "God's call to gentleness isn't a call to playing the doormat. It is a call to a posture. It's a gentleness sourced in humility, one that fully understands what it feels like to be the fool who received a mercy he didn't deserve. And one that longs to deliver that same mercy to as many fools as need it in return."[3]

Gentleness is the fruit of the Spirit that yields. Giant yellow triangular sign obeyed, gentleness pauses, looks both ways and . . . waits for directions before proceeding. With kids. With work. With friendships. With a mate. With parents. And with what we do to become who we want to be.

Get Growing

1. The definition of *gentleness* given in this chapter probably seems nothing like what you thought gentleness would be. What preconceptions did you have about this fruit? How did those preconceptions shape your like or dislike of this fruit? Admit it: Were you really looking forward to this one?

2. Consider Jesus's self-description in Matthew 11:29 of being gentle and humble in heart. How can you embrace His model of gentleness as your own? Read through other examples of Jesus's gentleness in Matthew 21:5, Luke 22:42,

2 Corinthians 10:1, and 1 Timothy 6:11. Can you think of other references in Scripture that demonstrate Jesus's gentle yieldedness to His Father's will?

3. In what areas of your life have you seen God growing the fruit of gentleness, helping you to yield your desires to His? Now . . . tougher question: Where are you still wrestling for control?

4. As the fruit of gentleness grows in our lives, like a banana that easily bruises, we do become more vulnerable. What precautions do we need to take as we allow God to grow this fruit? Is there such a thing as being too gentle, too yielded—or yielded to the wrong thing?

Dear Jesus, I yield to You. You alone are my safety zone. Cover me with Your love and protection as I yield my choices to Your desires. Help me especially in those relationships where I long for others to be in relationship with You; in those places where I long for others to change their attitudes; in spots where I wish I was recognized and known for who I really am. I put all these realities in Your hands to accomplish what You desire. I yield my desires to Yours. In Your name, Amen.

"We were gentle among you, like a nursing mother taking care of her own children." (1 Thessalonians 2:7 ESV)

The fruit of Gentleness looks like . . .

- Measuring my words before saying them. (Stacy)
- Giving over my power for the good of someone else. (Barbara)
- Choosing not to use one's strength as a source of action. (Nancy)
- Handling life with care. (Meg)
- Holding a tiny animal or a small baby. It is an expression of being calm. It is not weakness. (Lonnie)
- Living empathy out loud. (Donna)
- Putting aside MY agenda in any given situation. (Dawn)
- Learning to respond to others' criticisms or shortcomings with less verbal volume. (Christy)
- Even-keeled in temperament. (Carol)

CHAPTER 12

Self-Control

Healthy-Mindedness

Orange. *The orange is perhaps the fruit that most symbolizes health. Its vitamin C is prescribed for treatment of everything from the common cold to a wrinkled complexion.*

It had been a loooooooonnnnng day. It was late. I felt drained, sucked utterly dry, like one of those cardboard juice boxes—except there had been about fourteen straws stuck in me, and everybody around me had been taking a draw all day.

And then came the requests . . . for a shirt to be washed just after I'd folded and hung the last clean garment. For mac 'n' cheese instead of hamburgers. And—ooops!—for a dozen cookies for the bake sale, which no one had informed me was the next day.

I tried to hold it together. I took a deep breath. I thought about my "happy place." But somehow, the Monster Mom inside me snuck through a tiny hole in the wall around my emotions and made a break for it. She was out!

"IS THE MOTHER THE ONLY PERSON IN THIS FAMILY WHO CAN WASH A SHIRT?" she bellowed. Monster Mom wheeled toward the laundry room, snatching the soiled shirt in her grip and plunging it into the washing machine.

"IS THE MOTHER THE ONLY PERSON IN THIS FAMILY WHO CAN MAKE MAC 'N' CHEESE?" she screeched. Monster Mom slammed a saucepan into the sink, filling it to overflowing with hot water to boil. (Who was it that was boiling here?)

"IS THE MOTHER THE ONLY PERSON IN THIS FAMILY WHO CAN KEEP TRACK OF WHAT NEEDS TO BE DONE AND WHEN?" she escalated as she smacked a cookie sheet on the counter, attacking it with store-bought dough.

Yep, Monster Mom was on the loose, all right. Oh, I try to keep her pinned up inside. There is a thick, tall, imposing, and supposed-to-be-impenetrable wall about my inner being that keeps her in her place, unable to damage others or me. But sometimes she scrapes open a spot and escapes. I've discovered she's very resourceful. She can get through the tiniest of gaps. And if it's not Monster Mom, Wicked Woman will hiss her way out of hiding and into the world.

Is there a hole in your wall? Is there a spot where you tend to give way over and over again? Is it in the area of impatience? Imperfection? Temptation? Is there a tiny gap, barely noticeable, or even a gaping gash, through which all your good intentions hurry out?

"Like a city whose walls are broken through is a person who lacks self-control," says Proverbs 25:28. In ancient days, a city's wall protected the town against invasion by enemies. Even a small opening in the wall left the entire city vulnerable to attack. And that is why self-control is so important. Like a wall that hems us about, it protects us from losing ground to impatience, bitterness, greed, and pretty much any other kind of "ugly" that wants to take over our beings.

Most literally, the Greek word for "self-control" comes from two roots, one meaning to rein in or curb and the other meaning to heal, save, or make whole.[1] These roots apply particularly to our sensitive nature, our understanding, and our mind. Thus, to be self-controlled is to be "healthy-minded." Self-control is a healthy-mindedness that watches for the holes in the walls of our life and keeps them patched.

We're late getting the kids to bed because we couldn't tear ourselves away from the latest reality show finale. We're twenty pounds overweight, yet although our clothes are too tight and we're way uncomfortable, we down another bag of chips and salsa. The credit card balance creeps up and up, but we go ahead and get one more pair of shoes at the mall. We meant to finish the scrapbook laid out in the basement, but . . . We planned to get up a half-hour early to spend a few minutes alone—just for me time—with God, but . . .

Like the first in a row of dominoes giving way, a hole appears in the wall about our lives, and it grows larger with each temptation until it gives way to a gap big enough for Monster Mom, Shopaholic, Bad Mama, Wicked Woman, and the like to burst through. Pretty soon we're too weary to fight. Whatever. The hole's just too big now. Let it rip!

You relate. Ann confesses, "God is helping me to say no to things that are not good for me, but there are still days I fail miserably here." Christy admits, "Self-control seems to get harder the older I get!" Cindy says, "The hardest part of self-control is to deny myself." Stacy grieves, "I do not have it. I yearn for it. I feel this is totally broken in me, especially due to lifelong addictions."

It's never too late to repair the wall, though may seem so. One of the greatest lies in our days is, it's too late, it's too big, it's too bad, forget it. But self-control, like all spiritual fruit, is a fruit grown by God in our lives. And that means it's *not* too late today, and it won't be too late tomorrow. That's what's so great about God! He doesn't give up on us, so we don't have to give up on ourselves!

Now . . . what to do when there's a hole in your wall?

First, go back to the definition of self-control: healthy-mindedness. The holes in our walls are patched when we learn to think truthfully about our lives—in a healthy-minded fashion. What's the truth about who I am, and what I do, and what I want to be?

A life that matters is a life connected to God. If I'm connected, I'm growing in the fruit of the Spirit—love, joy, peace, patience, kindness, goodness, faithfulness, gentleness, and self-control—and that reality will produce, in me and through me, a life that matters.

With that in mind, next apply this healthy-minded thinking to all areas of life: your body, your relationships, and your purpose in life. Most of us unwittingly believe lies about who we are and our worth. Shaped by our upbringings, fed by the media's warped views, we swallow falsehoods and base our choices on myths. Self-control is a healthy-minded manner of thinking that helps us undo such crazy thinking.

What's the truth about your body? Is a model-perfect body the only "right" kind of body? On the other hand, is it healthy to just let your body blob out? What's the truth about your mind? Are you feeding it a diet of reality television myth? It's hard to be happy with reality when we're constantly gazing at fantasy. How about your expectations of yourself as a mom? As a single? As a spouse? As a daughter? When we constantly compare our offering to what other people offer, we find we're never good enough.

You get the drift.

It's amazing how powerfully unhealthy thinking affects us. Like a malicious prisoner sawing through our defenses, which daily protect us and keep us sane, unhealthy thinking begins in our minds and then escapes to affect our overall satisfaction with life.

Remember the orange, our symbol for this fruit of the Spirit. The orange is the fruit that most symbolizes health. Think healthy-mindedly. Apply healthy thinking to all the areas of your life. And keep it practical.

Start small. Pick one hole at a time to patch. Junk food. Screen time. Perfectionism. Don't try to tackle every spot at once. We do better when we build a series of small victories.

Keep disciplined company. It's so much easier to jog at 6:30 in the morning if you have a friend meeting you at the corner. Hang out with others who want to grow their lives and find strength in each other's company.

Work first and then play. If we try this the other way around, chances are we won't make much forward progress. We may even slide backwards.

Reward yourself. Self-control doesn't mean self-deprivation. Enjoy the good stuff when you reach a goal.

Consider seeking help. Many of us need professional assistance as we work through areas in our lives that seem out of control. There's no shame in therapy. It can be the key to great victory.

It's easy—tempting!—to misuse self-control. We can overdo it to the point of obsession. Or we can try to apply it to parts of life that aren't ours to control, such as our grown children's actions.

Self-control is healthy-mindedness. This is the fruit that patches the holes in the walls of our lives, protecting us from our worst temptations and desires.

"IS THE MOTHER THE ONLY ONE IN THE FAMILY WHO CAN FIX THE HOLE IN HER WALL?"

Yep, 'fraid so. At least, she's the only one who can recognize and own that hole and ask God to begin His restorative work in her.

Get Growing

1. Look around you. The ads in your social media feed. The displays in stores. The checkout line at the market. What messages about self-control do you encounter in your daily activities? How do these messages either shore up or break down your wall?

2. Memorize Proverbs 25:28 and recall it to mind as you take a walk around the wall of your life. Look for existing openings as well as spots that show signs of giving way, and list them out for yourself. Temptations. Emotions. Relationships. Attitudes. Addictions. Can you prioritize those that are most important for your immediate attention? What spots can wait? Before you set these spots aside, consider what damage might be done by a complete lack of attention. Now finish your prioritization and then set about patching through healthy-mindedness. Check back over the steps in the chapter as you get started.

3. Read other Scriptures that refer to self-control, such as Romans 12:2 and 1 Peter 1:14. How can your evolving understanding of self-control provide insight from these passages?

4. Is there such a thing as too much control? Why or why not? In what area of your life might this become an issue

for you? How can the growth of another fruit, such as joy or peace, help you to relinquish overcontrol in this area of your life?

5. How do you model the fruit of self-control to others? What would it look like for you to ask another person for prayer for God to grow this fruit in your life?

Dear Jesus, thank You for showing me where there are holes in the wall about my life. I know I can't patch all these holes without Your help. Please show me where I have believed lies about myself, my past, and my present and help me to replace these lies with the truth. In Your name, Amen.

> **"Be transformed by the renewing of your mind." (Romans 12:2)**

The fruit of Self-Control looks like . . .

- When I don't give in to my me-first attitude. (Barbara)
- The ability to do something or not do something because of Christ's inner nudge. (Becky)
- Shouting out a prayer for help before responding. (Caryl)
- When my flesh says eat a bag of chips, self-control limits me to a small bowl instead. (Carol)
- Learning when to practice yes, no, and not yet. (Donna)

- Being controlled by the Holy Spirit. (Gayle)
- Saying no to whatever catches me. (Steven)
- Asking myself, "What would Jesus do?" (Mike)
- Pausing, pausing, pausing. (Robin)
- Surrendering. (Colleen)
- Seeing self-control as a state of being rather than a checklist. (Jessica)

PART 3

Growing a Fruitful Life

CHAPTER 13

How Can We Evaluate Our Fruit?

How's the produce section of your life? Are your orchards yielding a good crop of God's fruit? Growing a life that matters means inspecting and evaluating our fruit.

I grew up in the 1950s and 1960s, when a popular decorative hack was to put out bowls with colorful plastic fruit as a centerpiece on the dining table or kitchen counter. No clue why fake fruit was seen as classier than the real thing—but for a season, it took over. Papier-mâché bananas. Realistically painted apples. The zany hues of the late sixties to match the wild wallpaper of the era.

Fake fruit can be pretty as an accent, but it does little to offer the real sustenance our world craves.

I've had my share of fake-fruit days. You know—mornings when I'm growling at my husband in the bathroom before either of us has even entered the shower. A gritchy mood while running errands that sends me into not-so-great interactions even with strangers. Once at a UPS mailing center, after hauling in box after box for shipment at Christmastime and getting a tart response from the counter worker, I replied in kind. As I exited, she remarked that she recognized me as a speaker at her church's retreat earlier that year. Great.

Fake fruit may pretty up a kitchen, but that's about it.

Jesus speaks to the difference between real and fake fruit in Matthew 7:15–18, 20: "Watch out for false prophets. . . . By their fruit you will recognize them. . . . Every good tree bears good fruit, but a bad tree bears bad fruit. A good tree cannot bear bad fruit, and a bad tree cannot bear good fruit. . . . Thus, by their fruit you will recognize them." I love how one commentator explains real fruit: "Fruit is not a *work*, i.e., something external from and perhaps disassociated from its source, but a *product* that corresponds to the nature of the tree."[1]

Are you living a fruit-filled life? Are your orchards yielding a good crop of God's fruit?

Love. Joy. Peace. Patience. Kindness. Goodness. Faithfulness. Gentleness. Self-control. The fruits of the Spirit are those characteristics that God produces in our lives when we're connected to Him. Their exact expression will vary a bit from personality to personality, but basically the fruits are those qualities we possess when we look like Jesus. Fruit makes us better than we would be otherwise. It empowers us to extend ourselves to others in ways that make a difference. Spiritual fruit markets God's nature to the world around us. The Gardener responsible for growing these fruits in our lives is God, although we must cooperate with Him in the growing process. Growing the fruit of the Spirit in our lives results in a life that matters in us and in all that we invest in our world.

So, how's it going . . . er, uh, growing, I should say? What kind of stuff is being produced in your life?

Hmm. "Can we measure spiritual fruit production?" asks Jan, among others. Jill steps back and ponders, "I don't know if I can measure it or should measure it." And Joan responds,

"You can't always. More often than not we don't even know the seeds we sow."

I love the honesty here! Let me suggest two elements that can help us measure spiritual fruit production: quality and quantity. Let's take them one at a time.

Quality. Are you growing genuine fruit that authentically represents God? Fake fruit offers an empty promise. It looks like real fruit. Often it even feels like real fruit—or better! But under the pressure of adversity, it dissolves. Fake fruit offers a feast for the eye while starving the stomach.

Oh, but it's so popular! Indeed. In place of love, we choose lust. Joy is replaced by temporary happiness. Peace trades places with contentment. Patience never buds; instead, a fake, smiley niceness takes over and cuts off hard relationships. Kindness mutates into manipulation. Goodness is good-enough-ness. Faithfulness is a suck-it-up steadiness of our own making. Gentleness is becoming a pushover. Self-control is ritualistic compulsivity.

Bite into that. (And then spit it back out.)

You know what it's like, this fake variety. "Sure, I can find time to take your kids—I love spending time with them!" (When you can't and you don't.) Or, "Oh, honey—I'd love to help you out, but I'm sooo busy with this project right now!" (When you wouldn't and you're not.)

One woman I know talks of "Beauty Pageanting" (in reference to the stereotype). It means putting on an artificial smile and saying everything's "just fine" when our world may be falling apart. That approach might feel comfortable, and maybe it's "nicer," but there's nothing spiritual about it. And it's not like Jesus.

Fake fruit is not the real thing. And it can't substitute for true spiritual fruit. There's no way to fake it. Pinch gentleness and its skin will bruise. Hack open patience and you'll find it sticking with you. With true goodness, what you see is what you get.

And self-control experienced in one arena brings the benefit of healthy-mindedness to every area of life.

Spiritual fruit doesn't have to be dressed up to be better. It's honest. It can say, "Oh, I'd like to help but I'm so exhausted!" or "Honey, is there any way I could do it this afternoon rather than this morning? Because then I'll be finished with my project." Spiritual fruit is not always available, or happy, or in a good mood, or pretty. But it does rise up out of the roots of dependency on God and tries its best—honestly, purely, and openly.

Spiritual fruit is the real deal. In initiating Jesus's ministry, John the Baptist exhorted, "Produce fruit in keeping with repentance" (Matthew 3:8). And years after Jesus's death and resurrection, James wrote, "The wisdom that comes from heaven is first of all pure; then peace-loving, considerate, submissive, full of mercy and good fruit, impartial and sincere. Peacemakers who sow in peace reap a harvest of righteousness" (James 3:17–18). How can you measure your fruit production next to these qualities?

Beware of fake fruit that offers the benefit of the real thing but delivers nothing. Check out the quality of your life's produce section.

Next? *Quantity.* The fruit of the Spirit is intended to present as a cluster. It grows in bunches. Together. If you find a picked-apart cluster, a vine adorned with a few measly fruit, you may have settled for selective fruit growing. Love. Gentleness. Self-control. Yep, those are there. But very little joy. Patience is stunted. Kindness, goodness, and faithfulness—check. But in the spot where peace should be displayed, zip.

God intended His fruit to grow in clusters of characteristics—all nine at once. And maybe even more. When He's growing an example of what He looks like, He strives to illustrate all the aspects of His nature, not just the ones that tend to spring naturally from certain types of personalities.

How are we to grow *clusters* of God's fruit? Some days, the best I seem able to offer is a fake-fruit response. It's all I can muster in the edgy atmosphere of my kitchen. More than a fake is more than I can manage.

We need to remember that it's not about what we can muster and manage. Spiritual fruit grows in our lives by God's initiative as we cooperate with Him. It's not up to us to grow all the fruit all at once all the time. But we can cooperate by recognizing where we're missing a fruit God would like to exhibit in our lives, or where we're faking it in our own strength, and intentionally asking God to produce it in us.

Let's go back to peace. Not there? Peace is resting in God in all circumstances. You're doing okay with this fruit when things in life are not irritating or upsetting, but today . . . well, life is exactly the opposite. Your mom just called to say she can't keep your kids because she has to go to the doctor. She's found a lump in her breast. Between your own schedule mishap and eruptions of terror and concern for your mom, your heart is as unruly as a bucking bronco on the plains of Wyoming. Peace? That's supposed to be resting in God, right? You can't even sit. Other fruits show up. Love is there . . . in everything. It's thick about you. Self-control appears; its healthy-mindedness holds you back from a moment of Monster Mom rage. But peace? Nope.

A quantity check reveals where fruit is missing. When we see the absence of fruit, we can ask God to make it present. May sound simple, and it really is. When we recognize that we don't have a certain fruit in our lives, our only job is to say so to God and ask for help. Pause. Pray. Remember it's not all up to you. Cooperate with the Gardener. It's His job to bring the growth.

Quality and quantity are the measurements we can use to evaluate the produce section of our lives.

Get Growing

1. Love. Joy. Peace. Patience. Kindness. Goodness. Faithfulness. Gentleness. Self-control. Each one of us more naturally exhibits some of these qualities while missing others. When we don't "get" a certain fruit, we might try to manufacture it ourselves.

    Look through the list of spiritual fruit for the presence of fake replacements, and name those replacements. What does a particular fake version look like in your personality? How does it show itself in your interactions with your children? Your friends? Your husband? Your coworkers?

2. Read James 3:17. How do the fruits of the Spirit you see in your life compare to these qualities?

3. What about the quantity question? Are there certain fruits that are simply absent in your days? Not just fake replacements but absent altogether? Name them. Now revisit the chapters of these fruits for an update on what you can do in order to cooperate with God's growth of them in your life.

Dear Jesus, thanks for helping me to see where I struggle with fruit production, both by settling for fake fruit and by ignoring the need for some varieties altogether. I recognize the absence of _____ and _____ in my life, and I acknowledge that I can't produce them by myself. They are a result of Your work in me. So I invite You to grow me! In Your name, Amen.

"Do not think of yourself more highly than you ought, but rather think of yourself with sober judgment, in accordance with the faith God has distributed to each of you." (Romans 12:3)

I can evaluate my fruit production by . . .

- Asking my accountability partner how I'm doing. (Gayle)
- Asking myself if what I'm doing would be pleasing to God. (Lisa)
- Keeping a journal. Looking back on certain incidents has a huge impact on my journey as I see where I failed and succeeded. (Michelle)
- The Holy Spirit shows us. (Tonya)
- How I act when trials and hard circumstances come, such as when someone treats me badly. (Ann)
- I think fruit is measured by how people talk about you— what qualities are you best known for? (Carol)

CHAPTER 14

How Do We Grow Fruit in All Seasons?

There are times when fruit seems to effortlessly fall off the trees of our lives. Abundant. Lush. Everywhere. Ever-present. You've experienced such seasons. They may be a bit rare for me, but I have too. Like the season of my father's death. I was a mother of young children in elementary school, I headed up MOPS International (now The MomCo), and my father lived two thousand miles away from me, yet somehow life *worked* so I could be where I needed to be when I needed to be there—and with a fruit-filled attitude. I remember helping with homework sans Monster Mom moments, making sack lunches, turning in a report for the office, climbing on a plane that arrived on time, and sitting prayerfully by my father's bedside, all in the space of a single day. It wasn't exactly easy. I was sad and concerned. But through it all, I experienced the peace of resting in God, the joy that arises from confidence that He was present even in those difficult days, and patience with all kinds of people and their bumpiness. Fruit grew in my life and from my life, and it offered sustenance to those around me.

Yes, there are such incredible moments, months, even seasons when fruit seems to pop out and plop into the laps of our lives and the lives of those we love.

And then there are other moments when *nothing* seems to bud. The branches of our days are bare. If juice is flowing through our trunks, we wouldn't know it. We plant ourselves in a relationship with God and wait.

That's been my experience. When, I wonder, will I look more like love, joy, peace, patience, and so on and less like . . . well, like me? I wake. I work. I wash. I worry. And I look pretty unfruity by the day's end. When will the fruit that makes God visible in me grow?

I know you wonder too. Fruit can come and go. Amy recognized that "the newborn phase of motherhood tested the growing of certain fruits, yet at the same time made easy growing of others." Dee noticed, "It was easier to grow in patience and faithfulness during past health issues. It was easier to wait on Jesus to act because of my faithful outlook that healing would come if I was patient." Elizabeth revealed, "Thirty years ago I was in church but not. I still thought I needed a man in my life to complete me. Well, I did—Jesus! From then on, I've been growing and still am!" Jan shares, "Gentleness is easy when the kids are little and innocent. Not so easy when they are grown adults who aren't doing what you want them to do."

Not seeing much in our own lives, we look to the lives of our children and grandchildren. When will the seeds we've planted grow fruit in them? There's the struggle in toddlerhood when every toy is sacred and none can be shared with a playmate. Mercy! Then in kindergarten we watch our child develop compassion for a friend whose daddy is sick. How precious! However, when it comes to his own strep-ridden little brother, no more Mister Nice Guy. Instead, he whines over why he can't hold the remote control, why he can't sit on Mommy's lap, and why he has to have soup instead of mac 'n' cheese. Later, in middle school years, just as we catch a glimpse of what might become fruit, out pops something that looks like a scraggly weed instead.

I remember a kindergarten gardening lesson from my own life. My teacher passed out paper cups and troweled dirt into each. Then we were given a few seeds to press into the dirt, followed by a bit of water. I carried my cup home, pulled a kitchen chair over to the windowsill, climbed on it, and set the cup on the sill. Every morning I repeated my climb to peer into my little garden only to find brown dirt in a cup.

One day I asked my mom if I could dig up my seed to see what it was doing in the dark. She replied, "Sure, but if you do, it will stop growing."

So much of fruit production can look like brown dirt in a cup. There are stagnant seasons when growth is invisible in our lives and the lives of those we love. In nature, this is called dormancy. In winter, look out your window at the bare-branched trees, or if you live in the desert, the flowerless cacti. Not much seems to be happening in dormancy.

Dormancy in fact increases a tree's yield—but only by quieting it first.

In some cases, dormancy is a response to external conditions—too much cold, not enough water, the need for more sun. Similarly, external stress may slow our personal fruit production. Joy seems less present. Patience? When we're attacked from the outside, it evaporates. Yet all the while, growth continues beneath the surface, and when conditions improve, fruit returns.

Diane shares from her own experience. "Fruit only comes when I am willing to relinquish all to Him and let Him do the watering, pruning, and growing. I have found that it is in the most difficult, tumultuous times of my life, when I feel like nothing is happening, that God shows me through it all that then and there is where the greatest and most luscious fruit bursts forth from the vine!"

How do we grow fruit in *all* of life's seasons—easy and hard?

An image from the Old Testament helps here. The prophet Jeremiah is speaking to the nation of Israel about their need to depend on God to grow them. (Sound familiar?) He says, "Blessed is the one who trusts in the LORD, whose confidence is in him. They will be like a tree planted by the water that sends out its roots by the stream. It does not fear when heat comes; its leaves are always green. It has no worries in a year of drought and never fails to bear fruit" (Jeremiah 17:7–8).

See how the tree is dependent on the stream, day in and day out, season to season? Because of such a relationship, it grows fruit eventually, regardless of its immediate condition. God's job is to grow fruit in our lives in all seasons. Our job is to be in a relationship with Him, like a tree is in relationship with streams of water.

What does it mean to be in such a relationship? Two simple principles emerge from this metaphor.

First, trees are planted. Being in a relationship with God means deciding to plant yourself in a connected place with Him. We talked about this at the very beginning of the book. The fruit of the Spirit grows only when we are connected with God in a relationship with His Son, Jesus.

Jesus's words in John 15:1–5 echo this dependency. "I am the true vine, and my Father is the gardener. He cuts off every branch in me that bears no fruit, while every branch that does bear fruit he prunes so that it will be even more fruitful. You are already clean because of the word I have spoken to you. Remain in me, as I also remain in you. No branch can bear fruit by itself; it must remain in the vine. Neither can you bear fruit unless you remain in me.

"I am the vine; you are the branches. If you remain in me and I in you, you will bear much fruit; apart from me you can do nothing."

If this is a step you've skipped, skip it no more. Go directly to the "Get Growing" section at the end of this chapter and walk your way through what it means to be planted in a relationship with God.

Second, trees send out their roots by the stream. The phrase "sends out its roots by the stream" implies that we hold on to God for our support, for our hope, and for our energy. Practically speaking, we root into God for how we define ourselves as people in the goals we set and the difference our lives will make.

Pick up a Bible and read more about the life of Jesus. Take fifteen minutes at the beginning of your day to sit quietly and think through how the Gardener wants to grow His fruit in you and how you can cooperate with Him through the items you set down in your schedule. Ask a friend if she wants to join you in this journey, and set a time to meet together to talk about "how it's growing."

To grow a life that matters is to produce a fruit-filled life. Year after year, fruit grows when we, like trees, plant ourselves by streams of water. Send down your roots even in the dormant days and you'll see fruit ripening in the future.

Get Growing

1. Perhaps the concept of becoming a tree planted "by the stream" in a relationship with God is unfamiliar to you. Is this something you'd like to do? Do you want to send your roots into God, depending on Him to produce His character in you? Just a simple prayer to ask Him will begin a relationship: "Dear Jesus, I want to plant myself

in a relationship with You, 'like a tree planted by the water that sends out its roots by the stream.' Every day I want to depend on You to grow the fruit of Your character in my life. I know that is what will produce a life that matters. In Your name, Amen."

2. Are you in a season of obvious fruit production? Look about your days for evidence. Where do you see fruit growing in your life? How about in your children or grandchildren? And what about in your relationship with others who've been hard for you to love? Take heart! Noticing fruitful and productive moments in life fuels us to face less productive times.

3. If you step back from the dormant trees in your life, can you imagine what is happening beneath the surface? How can you apply the principles of God's job and our job in the growing process during dormancy?

4. Think through past dormant seasons in your life. Can you give an example of fruit that grew from what seemed like only a barren, lifeless tree? How does such evidence of fruit in past seasons help you endure the dormant seasons of today?

5. Read Psalm 1. What does this Scripture passage teach you about growing fruit in all seasons?

Dear Jesus, I want to understand Your perspective on time and growth. When I look at the dormant trees in my life, help me see beyond the barrenness to what You are growing there. Give me restraint so

I don't uproot the trees that are planted and thereby interrupt Your work. In Your name, Amen.

> "There is a time for everything, and a season for every activity under the heavens . . . a time to plant and a time to uproot. . . . He has made everything beautiful in his time." (Ecclesiastes 3:1, 2, 11)

We can grow fruit in all seasons by . . .

- Learning that there is always more growth in difficult seasons. (Ann)
- When I am open to receiving God's good gifts, I see fruit multiply and flourish. (Cindy)
- Peace has come with age. I can think of many years when I anxiously awaited events or circumstances that took away peace in my life. Today I feel that no matter what comes, God will provide. (Ann)
- Patience is much easier when you don't have needy children, aging parents, a spouse, and a job all vying for your attention. (Joan)
- With a family, love and joy are easier. (Meg)

CHAPTER 15

How Can We Leave
a Fruitful Legacy?

Can you name your great-great-grandmother or -father? Er, uh, me neither. It's sobering to think we are remembered for only three generations (unless fame or fable carries on a longer reputation).[1]

As I move toward my seventh decade in this world, I often wonder what lasting contribution God might make through my life. I'm grateful that I've been able to continue working. My achievements have had some staying power. My children are now parents. My grandchildren are maturing. I've been able to put thoughts and insights down in print and in media, where I hope they will offer hope and encouragement for at least a while longer.

But then what? What about when I can no longer achieve? What kind of legacy will I leave then?

In his last book, *Our Greatest Gift*, Henri Nouwen differentiates between our achievements and our fruitfulness. It is our character, he maintains—the fruit of God's work in and through our lives—that lasts. Just as Jesus's true legacy was only expressed after His death, so ours will remain as we are remembered by those we love—even if only for a few generations.

So how will we cooperate with God as He tills the soil of our being to create His legacy in our life?

The choice begins with opening my eyes in the morning. What will I do today? No—who will I be?

The choice. The decision. The direction of my heart starts with my first conscious thought. I want to grow a life that matters. In me. In my family. In my work. In the relationships that extend outward from me like rings around a pebble plopped into a pond. I want my life to have something to show for it. I want to leave a fruitful legacy.

Yes, the choice begins with the opening of my eyes, and I continue choosing as I push back the covers, place my feet on the carpet, and head toward the shower and the needs both within and without the walls of my home. It is a clear choice, but it is also a costly choice. I am tired. There are many distractions. But still I choose.

Today my life will be fruitful. I choose to cooperate with the Gardener as He sets about growing the fruit of His Spirit in my life. I choose to be planted like a tree by streams of water. I send out my roots by the stream. I invite God to make me who He always had in mind I would be: more like Jesus.

In spite of circumstances, I will keep perspective on how fruit grows. There will be cycles of abundance as well as dormant days, but time will bring results as I wait well and live fully. Eventually my life will produce fruit in all seasons, and that harvest will draw others to the hope and healing they can have in God.

That's what I choose: a fruitful life. A life that matters.

Love. Joy. Peace. Patience. Kindness. Goodness. Faithfulness. Gentleness. Self-control.

I will love. I will make a committed choice to be there . . . in everything, even when it is hard to love hard-to-love people.

I will joy. I will have confidence in God, no matter what happens.

I will practice peace. I will rest in God, knowing that God holds me in the storms of life.

I will reach for patience. I will hang in with people and their problems.

I will express kindness. I will meet needs with compassion.

I will model goodness. I will be like God, inside and out.

I will keep faithfulness. I will be true to God.

I will live gentleness. I will yield myself to God's desires.

I will choose self-control. I will depend on healthy-minded thinking for all the areas of my life.

Impossible?

No. I will resist the temptation to think all this is impossible. Even though I fail just minutes into my day, I will remember that cultivating the different fruits in my life is not all up to me. My job is to cooperate with God as He grows them. It's up to me to want this fruitful life, a life that matters, and to say so to God, over and over and over again. It's up to Him to grow these qualities in me and then through me, to show them to others who also want them.

I will offer fruit to my children and grandchildren from my own life. I will model the process of cooperating with God, not hiding all my struggles but rather allowing the people in my life to watch because I know there are lessons in my failures as well as in my successes. I will recognize the moments of abundant fruit production when all that I've prayed for my loved ones occurs in a fabulous harvest season. In the dormant seasons of their days, I will serve as a historian, recalling prior fruitions, and I will believe those I care for will produce fruit again when it is difficult for them to believe for themselves.

I will offer fruit to my spouse. I will model my yieldedness to God. I will remain strong in who I am, and yet I will soften as I understand my other's needs. I will be intentional about exhibiting the freshest of God's fruits in the most familiar of my relationships: my marriage. When it is tempting to settle, to give what is not best but rather what is left over from other efforts, I will hold myself to giving from the firstfruits of my energies to the one I have pledged to love above all others.

I will offer fruit to my parents. While they may not have made this offering to me as a child growing up, I will choose to extend these qualities to them. While they may not share my faith or my relationship with God, I will not reject their journeys. I will value the investment they have made in me, and I will reciprocate the love they have always intended to give me.

I will offer fruit to my friends, my coworkers, and all whom I meet in my days. When I experience the temptation to measure out fruit to this person and not to that, I will hold myself accountable to the quality and quantity principles of fruit inspection. I will offer all the fruit to all I meet, allowing them to choose from my offering according to their wants and wishes. When I am wounded in life, I will choose forgiveness; I will make myself wise with my intentions, but I will continue to offer fruit.

I choose to grow a life that matters. I choose to offer fruit to those around me by seeking it for myself and then by modeling its production in my life, day in and day out. My life won't be perfect. I won't do it "right" all the time. I won't always look "nice" the way others think I should. But in the end, I pray that it can be said about me, "She looks like Jesus."

Get Growing

1. This chapter presents the reality of choice—considered and enacted each day. Look back over the list of brief "I will" declarations you just read on page 133. Are these your choices? Take a screenshot of them and keep it in your photo favorites to remind you often of what you've chosen.

2. Name five realities that get in the way of your choice making (such as time, busyness, distraction, weariness). How can you eliminate such issues in order to stay focused on fruit production?

3. Think back to chapter 10 on faithfulness. Just as God is faithful to produce this fruit in our lives, He is faithful to produce all the fruit of the Spirit. How can you lean into God's faithfulness in growing a life that matters?

Dear Jesus, I choose to cooperate with You as You produce Your fruit in me. I want to grow a life that matters because I possess qualities that look like You. In Your name, Amen.

"We know that when Christ appears, we shall be like him, for we shall see him as he is."
(1 John 3:2)

We know we are leaving a fruitful legacy when . . .

- Others say we have served and loved them well. (Amy)
- I get to heaven and God gives me a big hug. (Beth)
- My family and sphere of influence will speak evidence that my life mattered to them. (Christy)
- People see a glimpse of the goodness of God through me and what I have given as I have tried to live my life clinging to the One who has grafted me onto His tree. (Cindy)
- Jesus says so! (Dawn)
- I remember I'm not pointing others to me but that I'm made in the image of God and am called to reflect Him in my life. (Beth)
- I hear my son sing the same Scripture bedtime songs to his children that I sang to him. (Judy)
- I meet God and He says, "Well done, good and faithful servant." (Karen)
- My life is told at my funeral. (Kathy)
- The people I interact with, especially the ones I love and who love me, know Jesus better. (Michelle)
- My fruitful legacy lives on in those I leave behind. (Susan)

The Orchard

A Parable

How vividly I remember that Saturday morning! It started like so many others, but its ending was anything but expected. I'd been to town on errands and was returning home close to noon and ahead of schedule. So when I came upon the roadside fruit stand, I indulged the urge to stop. Under the canopies, bins of fruit wafted their tangy and sweet aromas, inviting me closer. With an ear-to-ear grin, the attendant handed me a brown bag to fill.

"Mornin'! Help yourself. Ya know there's no better fruit in the land."

I nodded in agreement. Indeed. I'd often stopped here and was never disappointed. Crisp, fresh apples. Oranges with skin so spongy they begged to be peeled. Pears free of the pockmarked blemishes of the grocery store. Cherries and strawberries in oh, so many yummy varieties!

"Ya know, they're all grown right here in The Orchard—right over the hill." The attendant pointed.

Following his gesture, I saw a simple wooden plank nailed crossways to a fencepost that read "The Orchard." I'd never noticed it before—stopped at this fruit stand umpteen times in the past year and yet somehow had overlooked that sign.

"Really? All this fruit is grown right here?" I asked, surprised. How could that be?

"Sure nuff. The Orchard Keeper can grow anything. Go see for yourself if you like." He pointed again beyond the sign to a path winding through the grass. "Hike on up and see where this fruit is grown. You can meet the Orchard Keeper for yourself!"

Meeting the Orchard Keeper

Why not? I set out down the trail, glancing back briefly at the attendant, who grinned again and nodded his head encouragingly. At first the path appeared seldom used, but the footing got easier as I climbed the hill. It was a steep hill, and as I crested it . . . well, I'll never forget the view that unfolded before me. The sight stopped me in my tracks. The neat rows of fruit trees stretching out over the countryside for miles.

The Orchard.

I didn't know much about fruit trees, but the sunlit colors sparkling amid green leaves before me spoke of apples, pears, peaches . . . and oranges. And were those *bananas*? And next to the trees, rows of vines and the prickly heads of . . . pineapples! Really? What an unlikely combination! Impossible!

As I stood there taking it all in, a figure stepped into a clearing between the trees. He was dressed in jeans and a white T-shirt, and he wore tan leather work gloves, but his head was bare to the sun. He carried a rake, a hoe, and shears, and a bolt of twine stuck out of his back pocket. Approaching me, he met my gaze, and his mouth broke into that same open grin as the attendant's back at the fruit stand.

"Hello!" he said, striding toward me. "Welcome to The Orchard."

He swept his arms wide across the far-reaching landscape. "What brings you here?"

A simple question. Why had I come? "Well, I guess I came to see where the fruit comes from," I stammered. "I mean, I've stopped here for years to buy it but never before noticed the sign, and, um . . . well, do you really grow this incredible fruit—all of it—right here?"

"Yes, I do."

"Apples and oranges and pears and even bananas, and so much more, all in one orchard? How is that possible? I could never do that!" My mind swirled at the thought of all the sweat, smarts, and money it would take.

"No, I don't imagine you could. But with me, everything is possible. I can grow anything. I'm the Orchard Keeper."

I didn't know what to say. His words sounded grandiose, but in his eyes I saw a humility I'd rarely encountered. He wasn't bragging, just telling the truth. I was even more interested.

The Orchard Keeper beckoned me to follow him into the trees. "See, I mapped this orchard out specifically to contain a variety of fruit. One type wasn't enough—no; I think a selection is important. All folks don't like the same kind of fruit, you know. Some are into citrus, others prefer stone fruit, and still others are fond of the classic apple or pear. So I make sure my orchard grows all types of fruit for all types of people. And I make sure my fruit is the best it can be—from the skin to the seed. The *best* fruit. All varieties of fruit. That's what my orchard is about, so that folks will come to the Source of all that fruit. That's what brought you here, isn't it—the fruit?"

Yes. It was the fruit that beckoned me to stop at the stand, to notice the sign, to follow the path up the hill and discover The Orchard, and now, finally, to meet the Orchard Keeper.

The Orchard Keeper smiled. "This isn't the only orchard around, you know," he said.

An Unlikely Orchard

What? I'd lived in the area for years. I couldn't think of a single orchard between here and my own property.

"Where?"

"Well, right in your own neighborhood—in fact, on your own parcel if I'm not mistaken. And I'm not—mistaken, that is. Your own land was intended as an orchard."

Mentally I inventoried the meager offerings of my landscape. There were those two scraggly pear trees on the left side of my lot. A measly, bug-infested stand of cherries. A few apple trees that still produced. Oh—and I'd staked up a potted lemon tree I'd carried back from vacation in Florida. I was rather proud of that little lemon tree, as I'd actually coaxed a fruit or two from its branches. But an orchard? Hardly.

The Orchard Keeper went on as if I'd been speaking out loud. "With the right care, those pear trees of yours would produce. Same with the cherries. And the apples are already quite productive, if I'm not mistaken—and I'm not. Yes, with some pruning, care, and a few lessons taken to heart, your trees will produce fruit beyond your imagination."

How did he know all this about my trees? "And the lemon?" I couldn't resist.

"Well, now, we'll have to talk about that lemon." He smiled. "Want to take a look? Want me to come with you and show you what I can do with your orchard?"

Why not? This had become a day of why nots. We made our way back down the path, past the smiling attendant, and got into my car. "You sure you have time for this?" I asked as I started the engine.

"It's what I do," he said as he settled in next to me.

Epilogue

Land Management

As we pulled into my drive, I cringed to think of the disarray. But gathering my best outlook, I braced myself for a quick tour. The Orchard Keeper followed me about my property, surveying my holdings. Then after we had completed our circuit, as we stood side by side, he looked at me intently. "Okay. You brought me here to your property. For years, you've done what you wanted with it, and now you have . . . well, you have this"—he gestured broadly—"to show for it. Are you satisfied with what you've accomplished? Is this what you want from your land?"

His question was direct. Part of me wanted time to think about my response. Lots of time. Of course I wasn't satisfied with what I'd accomplished! What did he think? But I had only so much time and energy and money to invest. I'd grown accustomed to the messy—and measly—result.

But . . . I looked over my land again, this time with new eyes. There were weeds everywhere. The branches of the trees seemed schizophrenic, sprouting shoots in all directions. Rotten fruit and damaged branches lay on the ground. Yet I also knew that on my front porch, sheltered by the awning, my little lemon tree huddled, clutching a single yellow fruit in its skinny arms. Perhaps my trees lacked flair, even begged for mercy, but the lemon was bearing. Not all bad.

Still, I knew where the Orchard Keeper was headed with his question. No, this wasn't what I wanted for my land. Surely his approach had to be better than mine.

Again he read my thoughts. "So you want more? You want to see what I can grow on your land?"

I nodded.

"Then you'll have to give me control. You'll have to surrender to me and to my ways. You'll need to allow me to be the Orchard Keeper that I am. Okay?"

I nodded again, even though I wasn't sure what all was involved in "surrendering." Soon I would find out.

The Pruning Process

"Let's get started." He headed first toward the pear trees. "Ah, these sweet trees," he said fondly. "But they're so much smaller than I imagined. Do they produce any fruit at all?"

"Er . . . not in the last few years," I murmured. They had produced in the past. I remembered my grandmother boiling their fruit into jellies and jams, canning the pears for Christmas gifts, and sharing them fresh with neighbors. But me? Well, I hadn't bothered much with them. Too much trouble.

"They'll need a good pruning," the Orchard Keeper said. I hadn't noticed the shears he'd been carrying, but now he pulled them out and set to work. "Could you get me a ladder from the garage?" he asked over his shoulder.

When I returned, ladder in tow, he'd clambered up the tree trunk and was lopping off branch after branch of diseased wood. The tree suddenly looked off balance, as if bitten by a hungry wind, leaving an unsightly gash in its foliage. I didn't like it.

"Don't take so much off," I objected. "You're making it ugly."

The Orchard Keeper paused mid cut and looked at me. "Every gardener knows that you hard-prune the weak shoots and light-prune the stronger growth. If you want fruit—healthy fruit and lots of it—I have to prune. If this tree had been properly shaped and trained when it was young, and kept that way, I wouldn't have to prune so much now. But there's so much damage. If fruit were to grow from these branches, they would break from the weight. Just wait. Come spring, it'll be worth it."

I took a step back and watched, hands in my pockets. The Orchard Keeper finished one pear tree and then moved on to the second, leaving them both looking scalped, vulnerable, and, just as I feared, ugly. I shuddered. What had I done, inviting him here? What would he do next?

Deep Root Feeding

I didn't have to wait long to find out. Setting aside his shears, he grabbed the ladder and headed for the cherries. There was a small stand of them, seven in all. Their shrunken leaves rattled in the breeze, mottled and shriveled. The Orchard Keeper's eyes went straight to the soil. Dry. He bent down and took a handful of dirt in his hands, rubbing it between his fingers as it spilled back to the ground.

"Get me a pitchfork, will you? And a hose."

When I returned, he began poking holes in the caked ground and softening it with water from the garden hose. "On second thought, this needs to soak. I'll leave the water running while we go to the next area and then come back."

Wall Repair

The rock wall around my property was originally constructed to keep out deer, raccoons, and coyotes, unwanted invaders that would strip my land of its produce. But my fruit trees' unproductiveness—due, sadly, to my own neglect—caused me to care little for the wall as well, and inevitably it fell into disrepair. What did it matter if the animals trespassed if there was so little fruit for them to steal? Apathy had replaced my once zealous passion for my property and its potential.

Until the Orchard Keeper approached the wall. And suddenly I remembered . . .

"Why is this storage shed here against the wall?" he asked. "It's so far away from the trees. How can it possibly be helpful? What do you keep in here, anyway?" His hand was on the latch handle before I could stop him.

The open door revealed the truth. There was nothing inside, only space leading to a larger opening, this one in the wall itself. See, the wall had begun to crumble, and for a while, I had diligently worked to shore it up. But one day it seemed like just too much effort. There were other things to do . . . and I had an idea. I decided to cover up the hole with a makeshift tool shed—a façade. In my mind, I decided a tool shed would look efficient and respectable. No one needed to know it was fake, just covering up the hole in the wall around my land. The hole I'd given up repairing.

But I knew the tool shed hadn't solved the problem. Later I discovered deer and even coyotes on my property. I wasn't really surprised to see them there, and I traced their tracks back to a growing gap in the wall behind the shed. All my efforts to repair that gap exhausted me. I'd invested time, money, and energy wheeling load after load of cement to slap up hasty patches that crumbled during the next rain or temperature change. I was fed up with the ever-widening gap.

Too much. Too big. Too late. While I'd grown accustomed to the hole, before the Orchard Keeper I felt ashamed, and beneath the shame, a profound sense of loss. I knew I'd settled. I'd given up on the discipline required to ensure safety, security, hope, and health for the rest of my property. As a landowner entrusted to provide for the land under my care, I had failed. I felt I *was* a failure.

The Orchard Keeper met my gaze. But instead of responding with judgment or disgust—or what I dreaded most, rejection—he gently offered, "I can fix this for you if you want me to."

I bowed my head and nodded. Relief filled my heart.

Within minutes, the shed was gone. The Orchard Keeper gathered the dismantled pieces into a neat pile, added the pruned pear branches, and set the stack ablaze. Next, he stepped through the gap into the wild and returned with enough rocks to repair the hole. He set them in place, smoothed cement into the cracks, and then, wiping his hands, smiled confidently at me.

"Remember this: there is no hole that's too much or too big for me to fix, and it's never too late for me to repair what has been ruined. Now, let's get back to those cherries."

The Compost Pile

After the soaking from the hose, the ground in the cherry stand was soft and ready to receive nutrients. "Sometimes the soil is too dry to receive the food a tree needs. Then the roots end up at the surface, like these. We need to remind these roots which direction to grow: down toward the water every day. Then they'll be able to transport the food required by the rest of the tree. Now a deep root feeding will net results in the coming seasons.

"But if it's a lush cherry crop we're after, we'll need more than food at the roots. Let's add a layer of food near the surface. Compost. Got any?"

What an understatement! In the far corner of my lot, an enormous bin overflowed with refuse. There were many days when I'd cynically concluded that the only growth on my entire land was that pile of garbage scraps.

"It does seem like a large pile of debris," the Orchard Keeper said, once again reading my thoughts. "Failures. Unfinished efforts. But such unwanted items, such discards from your days, can become the fertilizer for fruitfulness. Fruit production requires compost. In fact, the best fruit grows from layers of it. Come. Let's scoop up a few loads and lavish those cherries with promise!"

145

I'd never really considered the positive side of compost. I'd always seen it as refuse. But now, seeing it from the Orchard Keeper's perspective, what I'd defined as mere waste became purposeful. We grabbed a couple shovels, and in no time, we hauled several heaps from the compost pile to the cherry trees and layered the stinky but rich soil about their trunks. Then we stepped back and together evaluated our work. Yes. In time, the cherries would show the results of our labor.

Container Garden

I knew the Orchard Keeper meant what he said about fixing the holes in my wall. I felt hopeful and renewed. And then the cherry trees—I felt comfortable and confident in his direction for their growth. Time for a break, I decided, and I invited him into my house for some refreshment.

As we approached my front door, the Orchard Keeper noticed my lemon tree. "Ah . . . so this is the lemon you spoke of?" I nodded proudly. Maybe it was a little scrawny and weak, but it was growing a real fruit. I wasn't a total failure after all! Ta-daaa!

"I notice that you have kept this tree quite close to your house. You've sheltered it with the awning over the porch. You've staked it up in its pot here. I even see a hose curled up next to it and a spritzer bottle for keeping it moist."

"Yes!" I responded eagerly. "Aren't I doing a great job with it?"

"Well, you certainly are giving it effort—I'll agree to that. But take a closer look at your lemon. Is that what you're really after?"

I bent closer to examine the lone lemon. Its skin was puckered and uneven, and on the back side next to the branch where it hung, mold had gathered. A blush crept across my cheeks.

"The fact is that I never planted that lemon in your life. This fruit is of your own design and effort. At first glance it's attractive and winsome, but when you get closer, you catch the flaws. And all your effort has been invested here, in this self-selected fruit, rather than in the fruit I designed for your days. Besides that, it's clear that you intend to keep this fruit in its container. You have no intention of planting it permanently on the land I gave you. This fruit is adequate, but it's not mine."

Suddenly the lemon looked rotten to me. I had no desire for it. I realized I'd grown it out of my desire to control something for myself. I had brought it from another land, plunked it down in a container on my porch, and poured my total gardening efforts into it while ignoring the larger fruit production that was right under my nose. I thought it made me look nice; instead, I could see my effort was futile.

After a brief rest on the porch drinking lemonade—from a can, not made from the moldy lemon—the Orchard Keeper cast his eyes on the apple trees. They were next.

Good Apples

I thought the apple trees wouldn't be so bad since they were still producing fruit. I was wrong—that was the problem. They were indeed producing fruit. But it was all rotting on the ground.

The Orchard Keeper wasn't exactly angry, but there was no mistaking his disappointment. Squirrels fled as we drew near, grabbing what they could and scampering up trunks and into bushes. Abandoned apples remained in their wake, none fit for human consumption. Burgundy skin broke over yellow pulp that turned to mush underfoot.

"What a waste." Again, there was no judgment. Just the honest truth and attendant sorrow. I knew he was right. Why had I let all those apples go to waste?

I thought back to the hole in my orchard wall—and its lesson, which was all about my deficiency. On my own, by my own attempts, I couldn't fix the gap. The forces of nature were just too much. Too big. Too late. I'd given up . . . until now, as the Orchard Keeper encouraged me to invite *his* efforts into the fix. He could mend what I could not. And it was such a relief to surrender to his work.

So . . . what of the wasted apples? Now I could see it wasn't that fruit *wouldn't* grow in my orchard. The apples grew despite my lack of attention. And their very presence had intimidated me, for I had done nothing to merit such fruit. The apples represented undeserved good.

The Orchard Keeper looked at me and smiled. "You don't have to be good enough to grow fruit. That's my job. Your job is to cooperate with me as I grow fruit and to make room for it in your days. It's not about you.

"Now," he continued, "let's gather up what's left on these branches and box it up for your own fruit stand. What do you say?"

I hurried to the garage, where fruit boxes had been stored but never used, and returned carrying a stack of them to the Orchard Keeper. Together we pulled apples from their branches and nestled them in the boxes until we had packed almost five crates full to the brim. I climbed down from the ladder and surveyed the produce. Not bad. Not bad at all.

"No. In fact, very good!" the Orchard Keeper pronounced.

A Walk in the Orchard

"If you like, I will stay here with you and continue the work of fruit production in your land. I have ideas for some new varieties we could bring in right over there where the shed used to be. By this time next year, you could have many varieties of fruit for your own fruit stand down the lane. Folks like all kinds of fruit, you know.

"Between now and then, though, will you make a pact with me?"

My trust in the Orchard Keeper was growing. But a pact? I swallowed the lump that rose suddenly in my throat. "What kind of pact?"

"Just stroll with me. Every day, join me in the orchard of your land. Together we can take inventory of areas that are growing well and areas that need attention. And we can dream of new things to grow in new places. I like being with you. I want to hear your ideas. And remember, you don't have to grow fruit on your own. Your job is to welcome me into your land to do my work. My job is fruit production."

No more lump in my throat. I looked full into the Orchard Keeper's face, and my response was free and glad. "You bet. Produce your fruit in my land. *All* of your fruit in *all* of my land. After all, folks like all kinds of fruit."

Fruit Markets

It was a Saturday like so many before and so many since. A car pulled up at my fruit stand, and the driver emerged. His eyes surveyed the pears, apples, cherries, and, yes, even lemons in the bins about me.

"What beautiful fruit! Where does it come from?" the driver asked. I smiled and gestured at the sign to my side that read "The Orchard." He followed my gaze to the path next to the sign, then looked again at all my display. "Some fruit!" he said. "I'd like to see where it comes from. Mind if I explore?"

I grinned at him ear-to-ear. "Why not? Hike on up the path and see for yourself where this fruit is grown. Go and meet the Orchard Keeper!"

"But I say, walk by the Spirit, and you will not gratify the desires of the flesh. For the desires of the flesh are against the Spirit, and the desires of the Spirit are against the flesh, for these are opposed to each other, to keep you from doing the things you want to do. But if you are led by the Spirit, you are not under the law. . . .

"But the fruit of the Spirit is love, joy, peace, patience, kindness, goodness, faithfulness, gentleness, self-control; against such things there is no law. And those who belong to Christ Jesus have crucified the flesh with its passions and desires." (Galatians 5:16–18, 22–24 ESV)

Notes

Introduction—Longing for a Life That Matters

1. Bob Ginsberg, "How Long Will You Be Remembered?," *Beyond the Five Senses* (blog), December 20, 2020, https://www.beyondthefivesenses.com/post/how-long-will-you-be-remembered.

2. Ron Rolheiser, "Achievement versus Fruitfulness," Ron Rollheiser, OMI, September 4, 2017, https://ronrolheiser.com/achievement-versus-fruitfulness/.

3. Constantine R. Campbell, *A Fresh Look at the Fruit of the Spirit* (Grand Rapids: Our Daily Bread, 2014), 10.

Chapter 1—What Is Spiritual Fruit?

1. See Constantine R Campbell, *A Fresh Look at the Fruit of the Spirit* (Grand Rapids: Our Daily Bread, 2014), 9–15.

Chapter 3—How to "Get Growing": A Deeper Look

1. "What Are the Benefits of Pruning," *The Grounds Guys* (blog), updated June 1, 2023, https://www.groundsguys.com/blog/2017/september/the-importance-of-pruning-protect-your-plants-an/.

Chapter 4—Love: Our Always-in-Everything Commitment

1. Johannes Louw and Eugene Nida, eds., *Greek-English Lexicon of the New Testament: Based on Semantic Domains*, 2nd ed., vol. 1 (New York: United Bible Societies, 1996), 292.

Chapter 5—Joy: Confidence in God

1. H. Conzelmann and W. Zimmerli, "χαίρω, χαρά, συγχαίρω, χάρις, χαρίζομαι, χαριτόω, ἀχάριστος, χάρισμα, εὐχαριστέω, εὐχαριστία, εὐχάριστος," in *Theological Dictionary of the New Testament*, ed. G. Kittel, G. W. Bromiley, and G. Friedrich, vol. 9 (Grand Rapids, MI: Eerdmans, 2004), 369.
2. Ron Rolheiser, "One of Isaiah's Visions," Ron Rollheiser, OMI, November 27, 1997, https://ronrollheiser.com/one-of -isaiahs-visions/.

Chapter 6—Peace: Resting in God

1. Johannes Louw and Eugene Nida, eds., *Greek-English Lexicon of the New Testament: Based on Semantic Domains*, 2nd ed., vol. 1 (New York: United Bible Societies, 1996), 314.
2. "The Real Meaning of Peace," Melanie's Library, April 19, 2018, https://www.melanieslibrary.com/the-real-meaning -of-peace/.

Chapter 8—Kindness: Compassion in Action

1. Johannes Louw and Eugene Nida, eds., *Greek-English Lexicon of the New Testament: Based on Semantic Domains*, 2nd ed., vol. 1, (New York: United Bible Societies, 1996), 749.

Chapter 9—Goodness: Being like God Inside and Out

1. W. Grundmann, "ἀγαθός, ἀγαθοεργέω, ἀγαθοποιέω, -ός, -ία, ἀγαθωσύνη, φιλάγαθος, ἀφιλάγαθος," in *Theological*

Dictionary of the New Testament, ed. G. Kittel, G. W. Bromiley, and G. Friedrich, vol. 1 (Grand Rapids, MI: Eerdmans, 2004), 18.

2. Johannes Louw and Eugene Nida, eds., *Greek-English Lexicon of the New Testament: Based on Semantic Domains*, 2nd ed., vol. 1 (New York: United Bible Societies, 1996), 569.

3. Google Dictionary, s.v., "goodness," accessed March 7, 2024, https://www.google.com/search?q=goodness.

Chapter 10—Faithfulness: Being True to God

1. Johannes Louw and Eugene Nida, eds., *Greek-English Lexicon of the New Testament: Based on Semantic Domains*, 2nd ed., vol. 1 (New York: United Bible Societies, 1996), 378.

2. Louw and Nida, *Greek-English Lexicon*, 376.

Chapter 11—Gentleness: Yielded to God's Desires

1. Johannes Louw and Eugene Nida, eds., *Greek-English Lexicon of the New Testament: Based on Semantic Domains*, 2nd ed., vol. 1 (New York: United Bible Societies, 1996), 748.

2. "Strength Under Control: How to Lead Like a Meek War Horse," Matt Norman, February 6, 2018, https://www.mattnorman.com/meek/.

3. Michele Cushatt, *A Faith That Will Not Fail: 10 Practices to Build Up Your Faith When Your World Is Falling Apart* (Grand Rapids, MI: Zondervan, 2023), 72.

Chapter 12—Self-Control: Healthy-Mindedness

1. W. Grundmann, "ἐγκράτεια (ἀκρασία), ἐγκρατής (ἀκρατής), ἐγκρατεύομαι," in *Theological Dictionary of the New Testament*, ed. G. Kittel, G. W. Bromiley, and G. Friedrich, vol. 2 (Grand Rapids, MI: Eerdmans, 2004), 339.

Chapter 13—How Can We Evaluate Our Fruit?

1. James R. Edwards, *The Gospel According to Luke*, Pillar New Testament Commentary, ed. D. A. Carson (Grand Rapids, MI: Eerdmans, 2015), 205.

Chapter 15—How Can We Leave a Fruitful Legacy?

1. Jeannine Bryant, "In 4 Generations, We Will All Be Forgotten," Easy Rightsizing, December 12, 2019, https://easyrightsizing.com/in-four-generations-we-will-all-be-forgotten/.

Seek and she will find.

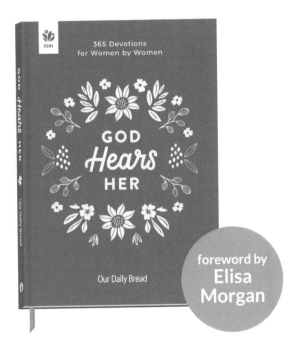

You'll be reminded that you are intimately known and deeply loved by your heavenly Father when you spend time with Him while reading *God Hears Her*. The personal stories, along with Scripture passages and inspirational quotes, reassure you that you are heard, cherished, and enough—no matter what you're going through.

Christmas changes everything—

THE COURSE OF HISTORY AND THE COURSE OF OUR LIVES.

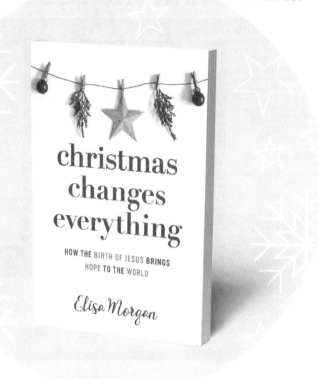

With the birth of the Christ-child, each person in the Christmas story experienced life-altering transformation— from Zechariah and Elizabeth to Mary and the Magi. Christmas can change you, too, as you learn to say yes to God with confident hope and true joy.

Order today

Do you struggle with loneliness?

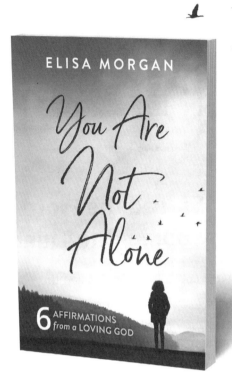

Feelings of loneliness can cause us to forget the truths of God's Word—that He loves us, gives meaning to our lives, will never leave us. Be encouraged, even in your darkest moments, by six affirming reminders of our loving God's person, plan, presence, provision, promise, and purpose.

Order today

Spread the Word
by Doing One Thing.

- Give a copy of this book as a gift.

- Share the QR code link via your social media.

- Write a review of this book on your blog, favorite bookseller's website, or at ODB.org/store.

- Recommend this book to your church, small group, or book club.

Connect with us. 🅕 🅞

Our Daily Bread Publishing
PO Box 3566, Grand Rapids, MI 49501, USA
Email: books@odb.org

Love God. Love Others.

with  Our Daily Bread.

Your gift changes lives.

Connect with us. 🄵 🄾

Our Daily Bread Publishing
PO Box 3566, Grand Rapids, MI 49501, USA
Email: books@odb.org